Bombings

by Gail B. Stewart

LUCENT BOOKS

An imprint of Thomson Gale, a part of The Thomson Corporation

THOMSON

™

GALE

Detroit • New York • San Francisco • San Diego • New Haven, Conn. • Waterville, Maine • London • Munich

Acknowledgement

We would like to express our sincere thanks to Jim Verdi, Special Agent Bomb Technician, Domestic Terrorism Squad, San Diego Division, FBI, for his invaluable review of Lucent's Crime Scene Investigations: *Bombings.*

LIBRARY OF CONGRESS CATALOGING-IN-PUBLICATION DATA

Stewart, Gail, 1949–
  Bombings / by Gail B. Stewart.
    p. cm. — (Crime scene investigations series)
  Includes bibliographical references and index.
  ISBN 1-59018-620-6 (hard cover : alk. paper) 1. Bombing investigation—Juvenile literature. I. Title. II. Series.
  HV8079.B62S74 2006
  363.25'964—dc22
                                                        2005026125

Printed in the United States of America

Contents

Foreword

The popularity of crime scene and investigative crime shows on television has come as a surprise to many who work in the field. The main surprise is the concept that crime scene analysts are the true crime solvers, when in truth, it takes dozens of people, doing many different jobs, to solve a crime. Often, the crime scene analyst's contribution is a small one. One Minnesota forensic scientist says that the public "has gotten the wrong idea. Because I work in a lab similar to the ones on *CSI*, people seem to think I'm solving crimes left and right—just me and my microscope. They don't believe me when I tell them that it's the investigators that are solving crimes, not me."

Crime scene analysts do have an important role to play, however. Science has rapidly added a whole new dimension to gathering and assessing evidence. Modern crime labs can match a hair of a murder suspect to one found on a murder victim, for example, or recover a latent fingerprint from a threatening letter, or use a powerful microscope to match tool marks made during the wiring of an explosive device to a tool in a suspect's possession.

Probably the most exciting of the forensic scientist's tools is DNA analysis. DNA can be found in just one drop of blood, a dribble of saliva on a toothbrush, or even the residue from a fingerprint. Some DNA analysis techniques enable scientists to tell with certainty, for example, whether a drop of blood on a suspect's shirt is that of a murder victim.

While these exciting techniques are now an essential part of many investigations, they cannot solve crimes alone. "DNA doesn't come with a name and address on it," says the Minnesota forensic scientist. "It's great if you have someone in custody to match the sample to, but otherwise, it doesn't help. That's the investigator's job. We can have all the great DNA evidence in the world, and without a suspect, it will just sit on the shelf. We've all seen cases with very little forensic evidence get solved by the resourcefulness of a detective."

While forensic specialists get the most media attention today, the work of detectives still forms the core of most criminal investigations. Their job, in many ways, has changed little over the years. Most cases are still solved through the persistence and determination of a criminal detective whose work may be anything but glamorous. Many cases require routine, even mind-numbing tasks. After the July 2005 bombings in London, for example, police officers sat in front of video players watching thousands of hours of closed-circuit television tape from security cameras throughout the city, and as a result were able to get the first images of the bombers.

The Lucent Books Crime Scene Investigations series explores the variety of ways crimes are solved. Titles cover particular crimes such as murder, specific cases such as the killing of three civil rights workers in Mississippi, or the role specialists such as medical examiners play in solving crimes. Each title in the series demonstrates the ways a crime may be solved, from the various applications of forensic science and technology to the reasoning of investigators. Sidebars examine both the limits and possibilities of the new technologies and present crime statistics, career information, and step-by-step explanations of scientific and legal processes.

The Crime Scene Investigations series strives to be both informative and realistic about how members of law enforcement—criminal investigators, forensic scientists, and others—solve crimes, for it is essential that student researchers understand that crime solving is rarely quick or easy. Many factors—from a detective's dogged pursuit of one tenuous lead to a suspect's careless mistakes to sheer luck to complex calculations computed in the lab—are all part of crime solving today.

An Unspeakable Crime

It was like a scene from hell. The bomb had gone off moments before, at 9:02 A.M. on April 19, 1995, and Oklahoma City's Murrah Federal Building was a ruin. Cable and concrete hung from the skeleton of the structure, and the sky was filled with dust and smoke. Glass blown from the building's windows was falling on sidewalks and streets blocks away. Cars near the building had been flattened like pancakes from the flying slabs of cement and metal that rained down on them.

"Black smoke was shooting in the air," recalls police sergeant Jerry Flowers. "I saw a car hood burning in the top of a tree. Debris, rocks, bodies, burned cars, glass, fire, and water covered Fifth Street."[1]

Confusion and Blood

There was an overwhelming reminder of death at the scene, too. Arms and legs that had been torn from bodies in the blast lay strewn in the rubble. People covered with blood lay on the sidewalk, some alive, others dead. "Out of the smoke the survivors staggered," writes one witness,

> some in their underwear, their clothes ripped off along with their skin, barefoot, walking over glass, covered in blood, dust, plaster.

> One man tottered down the sidewalk, blood on his face, declaring that he was heading home—only he didn't know where that might be, and couldn't remember his name. Others stumbled in shock, unaware they were hurt until they felt their shoes filling with blood.[2]

Rescuers (inset) work among the wreckage of the Alfred P. Murrah Federal Building in Oklahoma City in April 1995.

The building had housed a day care center, and frantic parents cried, asking if anyone had seen their children. Some children who had survived the bomb screamed, trapped in the wreckage or frightened by the dark smoke. Rescue workers, weeping, began bringing out the bodies. And across the nation, as the death toll rose to 168, including 19 children, and the number of injured surpassed 800, observers asked themselves, "Who would do such a thing?"

Surprisingly Not So Unusual

Though few bombings occur on the scale of the one in Oklahoma City, bombings are not an unusual crime. In the United States alone, between 1,500 and 2,000 bombings

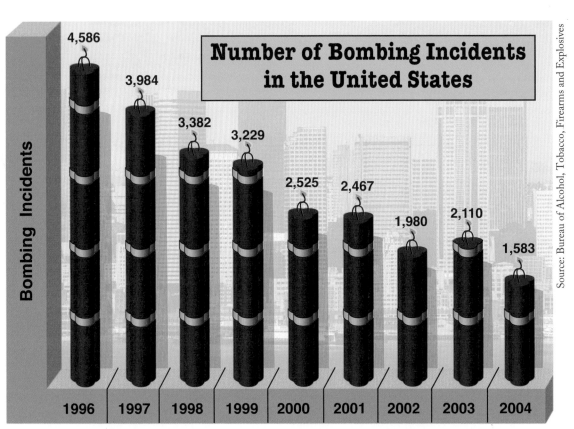

Number of Bombing Incidents in the United States

Bombing Incidents

1996	1997	1998	1999	2000	2001	2002	2003	2004
4,586	3,984	3,382	3,229	2,525	2,467	1,980	2,110	1,583

Source: Bureau of Alcohol, Tobacco, Firearms and Explosives

Includes bomb threats, stolen explosives, and thwarted attempts.

occur each year, killing more than 500 people. In addition, hundreds of would-be bombings are unsuccessful, either because of some technical malfunction with the bombs themselves, or because bomb squads are able to dismantle the devices before they explode.

Bombings would seem to be far more difficult to solve than other crimes, because by its very nature a bomb scene is reduced to pieces. Yet bombing investigations are frequently successful. "You look at the scene of one of the big, high-profile bombings, like back in 1995 in Oklahoma City, or the London bombings [of July 2005], and it's chaos," says Ron Kelley, an Australian security expert. "You have to ask yourself how anybody can even begin to solve those sorts of crimes.

British forensic investigators examine the remains of a bus destroyed by a terrorist's bomb in July 2005.

Where do those people who investigate it, where do they start? It's unfathomable—yet these investigators really have an amazing record of finding these bombers. That to me is pretty astonishing."[3]

Part of the reason for their success, say experts, is the wealth of technology that has become available in recent years—from instruments that can scan explosives residue on victims' clothing and identify the substance used, to closed-circuit cameras that occasionally capture an image of someone placing a bomb in a public place. Besides technology, investigators increasingly depend on the paper trail of bombing suspects for clues. A phone record linking a suspect with known terrorists, for example, or a receipt for material that could have been used to construct a bomb can substantially solidify a case against a bombing suspect. Even criminal profilers can provide investigators with valuable insights into the psychological makeup of someone who uses bombs to kill people and destroy property.

Generally, however, a case is developed by means of a combination of investigative tools, not the least of which is following through on every detail. "It's the little things that trip these criminals up," says one investigator working on the July 2005 London bombings. "The things these criminals don't bother checking, the little aspects of their tracks they neglect to cover—those are the things we have to check. In the end, that's the way we get these people once and for all."[4]

CHAPTER 1

Bombs from the Inside Out

All bombing investigators must have a full understanding of the way bombs work as well as specific knowledge about the various types of bombs that are used for criminal or terrorist activity. How a bomb is constructed, how it is detonated, and what types of explosives are used are critical pieces of information that can help an investigator track down a bomber.

A Chemical Reaction

A bomb is composed of three main parts that all work together to create a powerful chemical reaction. Some sort of power source triggers a device called a detonator, which then starts a chemical reaction in an explosive substance. The reaction happens when the chemicals within the explosive substance change, producing a high volume of gas that requires much more space than the container allows. The chemical reaction also produces intense heat and loud noise. The gases burst out of the container in a wave of pressure so strong that it literally rips apart anything in its path—walls, the sides of an airplane, or human flesh and bone. Pressure waves from bombs have been measured as moving up to 6 miles (9.75km) per second.

"That kind of pressure is a hard idea to fathom," says one bomb expert,

> especially in light of what most of us see on television. On TV, bombs are something people can escape from, which really isn't the case at all. My personal favorite is when the hero is standing fairly near a dangerous looking bomb, and at the second it goes off, he shields his eyes and leaps to safety—down a hill or behind a

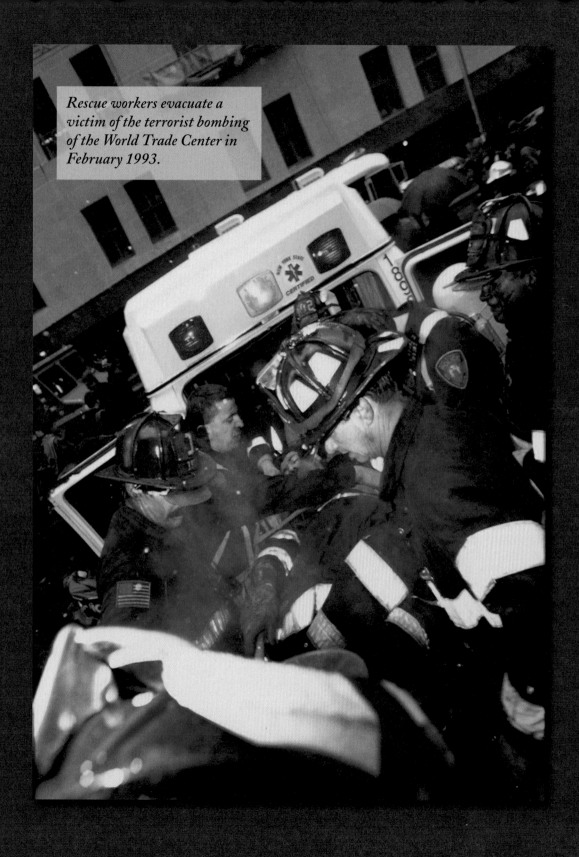

Rescue workers evacuate a victim of the terrorist bombing of the World Trade Center in February 1993.

tree. Or he leaps onto someone to shield them with his own body. That is utter nonsense. There is no way the human body can react faster than a bomb's pressure wave. [The hero] would have been dead before his brain even registered that the bomb had exploded.[5]

"The Force of That Bomb Was Phenomenal"

Dave Williams, an agent with the FBI's Explosives Unit, is someone who understands the force of a bomb's pressure wave. He witnessed the immediate aftermath of the bombing of the World Trade Center in New York City on February 26, 1993. The bomb, which was constructed of 1,200 pounds (544kg) of explosive, was packed into a large van that the bombers parked in an underground lot beneath the towers.

Just before the bomb exploded, the husband of a World Trade Center employee dropped off his wife and their infant son outside the building. When the bomb went off, the pressure wave ripped out a 3-foot-long (.91m) section of guard rail from the first basement level, mangled it into a 25-pound (11.3kg) metal ball, then flung it more than 300 yards (274m) up the ramp and up Vesey Street. Williams explains:

It shot through the rear window of [the employee's] car on the driver's side. It hit the infant seat where the baby had been seconds earlier, and if he'd still been there it would've killed him. It veered off between the bucket seats and embedded itself in the dashboard. If it hadn't hit the infant seat first, it would have taken the driver's head right off. The force of that bomb was phenomenal.[6]

By the Numbers

172

Number of residences bombed in the United States in 2004

A Range of Bombs

Many types of bombs are used in the commission of crimes. Most are homemade, with ingredients that are often available in any hobby or hardware store. "We are aware that just about anyone could make some sort of bomb," says one explosives expert who asked not to be named. "It's pretty much high school chemistry, combined with a lot of anger, I think."[7]

Molotov cocktails such as the one being thrown by this rioter are easily made using a bottle, gasoline, and a scrap of cloth.

Bomb makers use a wide variety of explosives. Gasoline is commonly used to make what is called a Molotov cocktail. The right combination of gasoline, a bottle, and a wick can produce a bomb that bursts into flame when it is thrown. In 1999 Molotov cocktails were used in the bombing of several Florida schools. Though no one was killed in the blasts, the explosions and fires resulted in millions of dollars worth of damage.

Gunpowder is another common explosive, and packed into a piece of plumbing pipe, it can be lethal. Pipe bombs are the most common bomb used, probably because they are easy to construct, relatively small, and made of readily available materials. A twenty-one-year-old college student named Luke Helder went on a five-day bombing spree in 2002, planting eighteen pipe bombs in mailboxes. When the supplies he used to make the bombs were traced back to a Wisconsin store, the manager explained that the purchases of pipe, tape, and other items raised no red flags. "We sell these products day to day routinely to hundreds of people," he said. "It wouldn't be anything out of the ordinary to notice."[8]

More Sophisticated Explosives

There are more high-tech forms of explosives, too. Semtex, made by a Czech company, is one of the most popular. This substance looks and feels like Play-Doh, and until recently it could almost always pass baggage checks undetected by airport screening dogs. (Semtex is now manufactured with a scent added, to discourage its use by terrorist bombers.) Developed originally as an explosive for construction companies, Semtex has in the past twenty years become the explosive of choice for many terrorists—primarily because so little of it is required to produce heavy damage.

One example is the bombing of Pan Am flight 103 on December 21, 1988. Just a little over 2 pounds (.90kg) of the explosive was packed into a small alarm clock that was then placed in a suitcase. The plane exploded over Lockerbie, Scotland, killing 271 people. Since that time the manufacturer of Semtex has tried to limit the sale of the explosive to legitimate businesses, but acknowledges there is a great deal of it on the black market. Nations with terrorist ties, such as Libya, Iran, and Syria, have all ordered hundreds of tons of Semtex in the past, and company officials have admitted that there is no way of knowing if the explosive is being used to build bombs.

Young Bombers

Explosives experts say that young people under the age of twenty-one are involved with making and setting off a sizable percentage of bombs. Because the ingredients for bombs are easy to get without raising suspicion, many juveniles say that they have made bombs in their garages without their parents realizing it.

"I'll never make another bomb," insists Cal in a personal interview with the author. Cal is a twenty-three-year-old who was arrested and spent time in juvenile detention after being caught setting off pipe bombs when he was twelve. "But there were a number of guys out where I lived—in the outer ring of the city—who made pipe bombs and set them off in people's mailboxes and sheds and stuff. It was a combination for me of being angry and bored and not having the brains to figure out something else to do."

Juveniles are also a growing source of bomb threats—actual or hoaxes—especially to schools. "More and more kids see it as a way to get some excitement, and maybe a day off from school," says one police officer, also in a personal interview with the author. "But most of them don't know that if they're caught, they can face very severe fines and detention time—lots more than just a slap on the wrist."

Cell Phones and Letter Bombs

There are a range of choices for bomb components, too. Many crude explosive devices go off when a lit fuse burns down to the bomb. Some large bombs, such as the one used in the Oklahoma City bombing, are set off by lighting a stick of dynamite. The powerful blast of the dynamite ignited the bomb, which was made of a combination of ammonium nitrate (found in fertilizer) and fuel oil.

But not every bomb is intended for immediate explosion by the bomber. In such cases bombers create a mechanism to delay setting off the explosive for hours or even days. Some bombs are built to be sent through the mail, such as those made by Walter Leroy Moody. Moody's bombs, placed in small packages delivered by the post office, killed an Alabama federal judge and a Savannah, Georgia, civil rights worker in 1989.

Moody's devices were pipe bombs that contained a timing mechanism made of batteries, parts of light bulbs, and other easily obtainable items. Says one explosives expert:

> Without going into much detail, I'll just say that a bomb can be detonated by simply completing an electronic circuit. A person can accomplish that with just about anything—timers, flash bulbs, batteries, even cell phones.

> For example, the terrorist bombing in Madrid [in 2004] was carried out using cell phones. There were backpacks or gym bags left on a number of train cars at morning rush hour, and they each contained 25 pounds [11.25kg] of explosive, which is surprisingly not very bulky. I mean, someone wouldn't necessarily be suspicious by its size or shape—it would just look like a standard backpack a high school or college-age person would use. Each of the bags contained a cell phone wired to the explosive material. When the bombers decided it was time, they simply called the number and completed the circuit.[9]

Cell phones can be used to detonate bombs, as in the 2004 Madrid bombings.

Insidious "Extras"

Although setting off a bomb is destructive enough, in recent years bombers have frequently added things to their bombs to make them even more deadly. For example, an increasing number of bombs contain shrapnel—nails, chains, marbles, or any other small hard objects. When the bomb explodes, the shrapnel is propelled outward, drastically increasing the likelihood of fatalities.

A bomb laden with shrapnel went off on July 27, 1996, at the Summer Olympic Games in Atlanta. Three pipe bombs were hidden inside a backpack and left at a media tower in the Olympic Village. Security personnel discovered the bombs and began to evacuate the area, but the backpack's contents exploded before everyone could get away. Alice Hawthorne, a forty-four-year-old mother of two, was standing 80 feet

Targeting racial and ethnic minorities, David Copeland (opposite) used pipe bombs packed with nails in a series of attacks in London like the one pictured below.

(24.4m) from the bomb when it exploded, and she died from extensive wounds caused by the metal shrapnel. More than one hundred other people were seriously injured by the projectiles.

In another case, David Copeland of London became known as the Nail Bomber because of his use of shrapnel. Copeland went on a twelve-day bombing campaign in April 1999, targeting racial and ethnic minorities in the city. His pipe bombs, each packed with at least 1,500 nails, were left in bars and businesses that catered to minorities. The bombs killed 3 people and injured 140 more. Police say that shrapnel was responsible for almost all of the deaths. One of the survivors was a two-year-old who was critically injured when the blast drove a long nail through his skull.

"It's Loud and It's Violent"

Though the bombs that rocked Oklahoma City, the World Trade Center, and London are well-known terrorist crimes, experts say that foreign or domestic terrorism is behind only a small fraction of bombing incidents. In other cases, bombs are used by fired employees as a way of seeking revenge. Gangs may use car bombs to kill rival gang members, and drug dealers who operate methamphetamine labs often set up explosive booby traps to kill or injure police making a drug bust.

Even though most bombers are not considered terrorists, investigators maintain that any bombing incident, whether committed by terrorists or not, is by its very nature a terror-producing crime. "It's loud and it's violent," says Kelley.

How can anyone nearby help but be terrified? I was in Warsaw [Poland] nine years ago when a truck was bombed—I don't know the reason. I was a block away—it's not like it was a close call for me, but the whole thing scared me to death. I couldn't stop thinking about it for weeks.

The truck exploded, and killed the two guys inside. No one else was killed, but the bomber didn't know that. The bomber didn't know who would be around when the bomb went off. He didn't know, he probably didn't think about it, or care. There could have been a whole crowd of people going by at that very instant, a bunch of kids walking to school or something. That's the violence of a bomb. It's unbelievably random. Whoever's around, they're victims just by being nearby.[10]

The Bombing of United Airlines Flight 629

Many people mistakenly assume that the bombing of airliners is a new phenomenon. However, experts say bombs began to be a threat on U.S. domestic flights on November 1, 1955. United Airlines flight 629 took off from Denver, and less than fifteen minutes later, exploded in midair. A bomb was suspected, and investigators subsequently found traces of dynamite on metal fragments recovered from the crash site. The motive was not terrorism, however.

The investigators did background checks of the passengers and found that one man, Jack Graham, had recently purchased several expensive travel insurance policies for his mother, who had died in the crash. In searching Graham's home, detectives found bomb-making ingredients. In addition, Graham's wife admitted that her husband had slipped what he claimed was a small gift into his mother's suitcase before the flight. Graham was convicted and sentenced to death.

JTTF

A bombing has the potential to result in hundreds or even thousands of casualties. Because of the catastrophic nature of explosions and the increasing use of bombs by terrorists, the process of investigating a bombing is done by highly trained explosive specialists. Although the first responders to any reported explosion are local police departments, once police suspect that an explosion was due to a bomb—rather than a ruptured gas pipe, for example—the JTTF (Joint Terrorism Task Force) will be called in to determine if the incident is related to terrorism. This 140-member group combines the resources of the FBI, the U.S. Marshals Service, the Bureau of Alcohol, Tobacco, and Firearms (ATF), U.S. Citizenship and Immigration Services, and other state, local, and federal agencies. The JTTF is intended to be a cohesive unit that can focus entirely on terrorist bombings.

But whether a bomb was set by terrorists or a revenge-seeking ex-employee, the first order of business for bomb investigators is to examine the crime scene. And that can be the most stressful, dangerous, and difficult part of the investigation.

CHAPTER 2

The Scene of the Bombing

Investigators know that unless they do a thorough search of the scene of a bomb blast, the chances are slim that they will ever solve the case. Careful examination is crucial to finding out what sort of bomb it was, what particular explosive was used, where the bomb was placed, and how it arrived there. Each small piece of evidence recovered from the scene helps form a larger picture that may lead to other clues that ultimately reveal the identity of the bomber.

Secondary Bombs

Although it is important to process the area thoroughly after an explosion, there are great dangers at the scene of a bombing. One of the greatest is a secondary bomb. Bombers—especially terrorist bombers—often plant two bombs. The second, heavily loaded with shrapnel, is to target police, bomb technicians, or medical emergency teams that rush to help the victims of the first blast.

A secondary bomb was set off on January 16, 1997, at a family planning clinic in Sandy Springs, Georgia. The first bomb exploded at 9:00 A.M. as the clinic was opening for the day. No one was injured. However, a second bomb went off a little more than an hour later, when police and firefighters were assessing the crime scene. Seven people were injured in that second explosion, several of them police officers.

"It Was Like Walking into a Bizarre Cave"

Even if there is no secondary bomb, the building where a bombing occurred can be structurally dangerous to investigators. The

Workers assigned to recover bodies go about this grim and dangerous task at the Alfred P. Murrah Federal Building.

In February 1993 a terrorist bomb ripped a gaping hole in the parking garage beneath the World Trade Center.

underground parking garage at the World Trade Center was a very unstable scene, recalls the agent in charge, Dave Williams:

> It was like walking into a bizarre cave. The explosion had ripped through five levels of the parking garage. Slabs of concrete as large as basketball courts, eighteen inches [45.72cm] thick, were just hanging in midair, and they'd suddenly break loose and fall several stories and the whole building would begin to shake. Steel beams were broken and twisted . . . [and] the building was still moving. We put a spacer in a half-inch crack [1.27cm] and walked a hundred feet [30.5m], and by the time we got back the spacer was gone and the crack was six inches [15.24cm] wide.[11]

Adding to the danger was the lack of light, since the electricity had gone out when the bomb exploded. In fact, the only light came from the flashing headlights of those cars among the sixteen hundred in the garage that had alarms. Finally, scores of broken pipes poured water and untreated human waste into the site. After rescue workers risked their lives to bring out victims, Williams insisted that the investigation of the scene had to wait until structural engineers were able to make an assessment of the crime scene.

Widow-Makers and Other Hazards

After the Oklahoma City bombing, the Murrah Building was unsteady as well, and agents in charge of the investigation brought in experts to assess the risks. Ray Downey, a former fire chief in New York City who had done an assessment of the World Trade Center after the bombing in 1993, found the Oklahoma scene even more hazardous. "I determined that the Federal Building had significantly more damage to important components [than the World Trade Center]," he said, "and was in much greater danger of further collapse."[12]

Nothing was stable about the Murrah Building, Downey observed. Huge concrete slabs, measuring 15 feet by 30 feet (4.6m by 9.1m), hung from the ninth and eighth floors. Calling them "widow-makers" because of the danger they represented, Downey was concerned that they could easily be jarred loose by wind or further movement of the building and would then come crashing down on investigators.

One of the ways the scene was made more secure was the installation of crosshair monitors that measured even the slightest movement of the ruined building. These monitors were so accurate that they noted that when the sun came out, its heat would make the east wall expand almost

By the Numbers

16

Number of people killed in bombings in the United States in 2004

one-half inch (1.27cm). Work crews paid careful attention to the monitors, and on more than one occasion sounded an alarm for all investigators to get away from the building when structural shifting occurred.

Finding the Crater

When the site is deemed safe enough, bomb crews begin their work. One of the first jobs is to locate the exact location of the bomb before it went off. A bomb in a structure such as the World Trade Center or the Murrah Building leaves a large crater below it. That is called the seat of the explosion, and its size can tell investigators the approximate size of the bomb. In some cases, as in Oklahoma City where the bomb was directly outside the building when it exploded, the crater is easy to see. In other cases, such as the World Trade Center bombing, the crater is not visible right away.

As explosives experts climbed through the tangle of shredded cars, concrete, and other debris in the dark parking garage under the World Trade Center, they relied on their assessment of the damage to find the crater. They knew that

A police officer takes notes as he examines a car destroyed in the February 1993 bombing of the World Trade Center.

the closer to the seat of the explosion, the more severe the bombing damage.

The cars in the garage provided that information. Though all the cars had been streaked with grime and dust from the explosion, the agents noticed that cars in one particular area were charred and in far worse shape than the other vehicles the crews had seen. Moving in that direction, they saw a huge crater, measuring 200 feet by 100 feet (61m by 30.5m) and sinking seven stories below the ground. Recalls one bomb technician at the scene, "We made the determination right there in the hole . . . that we had a large explosive device, probably a vehicle device, because there was no way somebody could carry in something that big and set it off."[13]

"If It's Not a Rock and It's Not Growing . . ."

In a case such as the bombing of Pan Am flight 103, however, there was no crater. The plane had taken off from London and exploded in midair over Scotland. Bodies, luggage, and other debris from the plane were strewn over 845 square miles (2,189 sq. km). Heavy crosswinds at the time of the explosion wrenched clothing and jewelry from bodies as they fell. For example, a watch from a body that had fallen in the farm area of Tundergarth was recovered in Northumbria, more than 80 miles (129km) away. The task was even more daunting because of the terrain below, which ranged from farm fields to thick forests and bogs.

To search the scene, British, Scottish, and American bomb technicians had a great deal of help. Soldiers, local police, and Lockerbie townspeople were eager to assist them. Fire officials used their hook and ladder trucks to retrieve bodies from the roofs of homes. Police distributed clear plastic bags for people to put any debris in. Local police, farmers, and townspeople aided in collecting the tons of material scattered over the

Scottish countryside. Volunteers who were unsure of what to pick up were told, "If it's not a rock and it's not growing, put it in the bag."[14]

At the World Trade Center bombing site, investigators told crews to collect everything. However, they soon realized that they should have been more discriminating in what they collected. It was, investigators later said, the first major bombing in the United States, and their lack of experience showed. "We didn't know what to collect and what not to collect," says bomb technician Don Haldimann. "So we erred on the side of caution and seized everything. We ended up with ten to twenty tons of stuff we really didn't need. We got explosively damaged wood, concrete, you name it. We didn't need all that stuff."[15]

Looking for Clues

One of the pieces of debris most highly valued by investigators is a fragment of the bomb itself. Experts say that it is a misconception that a bomb is destroyed as it explodes. Actually, almost 95 percent of it remains, although it is in very tiny pieces—some barely visible without a microscope.

Occasionally crews are lucky enough to find recognizable bomb fragments at the scene. At Oklahoma City, for example, a number of blue plastic fragments were discovered, and experts were able to identify them as pieces of large containers used for storage. They reasoned that these containers had held the large amount of explosive used in the bomb.

In another incident several bomb fragments were discovered after they had been accidentally removed from the scene. In 1976 a Chilean diplomat named Orlando Letelier was killed in a car bombing in Washington, D.C. His vehicle was extinguished by firefighters who drove through the crime scene in their haste to put out the blaze. Alert investigators visited the fire station later that night and looked for evidence that might have been wedged in the fire engine's tires. They recovered a metal pin that had been taped to Letelier's car to hold the bomb

in place. In addition they found part of a remote control device that was used to detonate the bomb.

Grids and Swabs

Although occasionally a bomb investigation may turn up a fragment of a bomb right away, such cases are the exception rather than the rule. In most instances, recovering bomb fragments is the result of a painstaking process. At almost every bomb scene investigators create a grid on a map of the site (or in the case of Lockerbie, the town and the surrounding area). That way they can keep track of where various debris is found. Knowing how far a piece of explosive-damaged debris traveled in a bomb explosion may give investigators an idea of the amount and type of explosive used.

At Lockerbie investigators divided the surrounding area into eleven sectors. As people brought in their collection bags, agents tagged and numbered the collected material and in the days and

An agent from the bureau of Alcohol, Tobacco, and Firearms (ATF) searches debris from the bombing of Centennial Olympic Park in Atlanta in the summer of 1996.

weeks that followed sorted it according to whether it was baggage, plane parts, or other matter. They were especially looking for fragments of the bomb or of the material that exploded around it. Though no such fragments were immediately recognized at the scene, the material was later "fingertipped"—searched and sifted through using finer and finer mesh screens until searchers were certain nothing had been missed.

Even though there may be tons of debris after a bombing blast, investigators say that locating the remains of the bomb and pieces of plastic or metal that were very close to it when it exploded is not as difficult as it is time-consuming. "Explosive damage has a very distinct look," says expert Tom Thurman of the FBI. "Bomb fragments will have jagged edges and they might be coated with residue and soot. Depending on the force of the explosion, they'll probably be a little smaller than debris resulting from a crash. If people know what to look for, bomb damage isn't hard to identify."[16]

As crews search the seat of the blast, some of them look for explosive residue by running cotton swabs over the walls or larger debris at the scene. The swabs are carefully bagged in an airtight container, such as a sealed jar, and taken to a forensic lab. There they are tested for a variety of explosives. The type of explosive used can be another thread for investigators to follow. As one explosives expert explains, "Anything that we can pursue is a good lead. A bomb may be homemade, but the materials have to come from somewhere. An investigator understands very well that if you know the 'where,' that can eventually lead you to the 'who.'"[17]

Valuable Vehicle Parts

In large-scale bombings such as the one at the World Trade Center, investigators say there is evidence that can prove even more valuable than bomb fragments—car parts. The vehicle used to bring the bomb to the site fragments during the explosion, and those pieces may lead investigators to the name of the individual who owned or rented it.

Investigators search for clues in the remains of a vehicle that was used in a bombing in Beirut, Lebanon.

As investigators Donald Sadowy and Joe Hanlin made their way to the seat of the World Trade Center explosion, they saw two car parts that were especially charred and fragmented. Sadowy was amazed at the damage to the metal. "This is forged steel," he told Hanlin. "Never in my life have I seen it ripped apart like this. To get blown apart this violently, they had to be sitting right underneath the bomb!"[18]

The men looked through the debris nearby and found a 4-foot-long (1.2m) piece of metal that turned out to be part of the rear frame of a vehicle. What made this fragment extremely valuable was the vehicle identification number (VIN) stamped on it. Every car that is produced is stamped with its own VIN. This number makes it possible for police to trace

Training Bomb-Sniffing Dogs

When bomb squads check a bombing scene to be sure that a secondary explosive has not been set, they frequently bring a dog trained to react to even the tiniest amount of explosive. In fact, such dogs can detect vapors given off by explosives in concentrations ten thousand times lower than those humans can pick up. Most of the dogs used across the United States are Labrador retrievers, chosen because their sense of smell is exceedingly accurate and because they are smart and easy to train.

Explosives-detecting dogs are trained by exposing them to twenty of the most common elements found in explosives. Some dogs are trained using food as a reward. When the trainer lets a dog sniff the element, the dog is told to sit and is given a bit of food at the same time. Soon the dog reacts to the smell by sitting—a posture that will alert a bomb squad handler that the dog has detected an explosive. During a typical day of training, a dog is exposed to explosives more than one hundred times and receives food each time.

Other dogs are trained using play as a reward. The trainer keeps a favorite toy at hand, and rewards the dog for detecting an explosive by letting the dog play with the toy.

Specially trained dogs are used at suspected bombing sites to sniff out residues left by explosives.

a car that has been stolen, even if different license plates have been put on it.

The VIN turned out to belong to a Ford Econoline van that had been purchased by the Ryder rental company. Investigators traced the van to a specific rental office and found the name of the man who had rented the van. In short order the man was arrested—one of many involved in the plot to bomb the World Trade Center.

Testing Explosives on Vehicles

Workers on the Dipole Might project follow this procedure to test explosives on vehicles:

1 **Technicians ready** four different types of roadbed types, ranging from dirt roads to paved highway. They create a grid system on each roadbed, assigning a number to each portion of the grid.

2 **A vehicle**—either a passenger van or a four-door sedan—is loaded with a set amount of explosives. The type and amount varies each time and is carefully recorded.

3 **Technicians position** several high-speed cameras, both video and still, so that they can record the blast from a number of angles.

4 **The vehicle's explosives** are detonated by remote control.

5 **After the explosion** technicians carefully note where each fragment of the vehicle landed. They measure its distance from the crater, or seat of the explosion, and mark it on a computer grid.

6 **The information** is entered into the ATF database so that it can be used in real-life bombings involving vehicles.

Dipole Might

Soon after the World Trade Center bombing, explosives experts recognized that it would be helpful to understand more about the behavior of bombs that explode in vehicles. Being able to predict how a car would fragment, for instance, would help investigators in the future know where to look for pieces of the vehicle.

For that purpose the ATF began a project, code-named Dipole Might, in 1993. Bomb crews at the White Sands Missile Range in New Mexico actually blew up various vans, cars, and trucks loaded with the types of explosives bombers would be most likely to use. After each explosion the vehicle's parts that survived the blast were marked on a grid, and this information was fed into a computer. The results showed what parts will survive a large blast and where they consistently land, depending on the size of the bomb.

Rescuers and FBI personnel comb the ruins of the Alfred P. Murrah Federal Building, searching for survivors and clues to the identity of the bomber.

Bombing Targets in the United States, 2004

33% Residences

20% Mailboxes

13% Vehicles

13% Businesses

10% Government offices and facilities

7% Schools

2% Other

2% Religious targets

Source: Bureau of Alcohol, Tobacco, Firearms and Explosives

Such information has proved helpful in other cases. In Oklahoma City, for example, agents were able to find pieces of the vehicle in a very short time. The vehicle's frame and axle broke just as they did in the Dipole Might tests and traveled in the direction experts predicted. The VIN was located, too, and just as in the World Trade Center case, the number gave investigators an invaluable clue to the bomber's identity.

Moving from the Crime Scene

When crews are satisfied that they have retrieved every piece of debris that could be important to the case, they move the evidence to various laboratories and examination rooms where it can be scrutinized more closely. While some investigators concern themselves with this material, others begin their examination of the human crime scene—the victims themselves.

CHAPTER 3

Identifying the Dead

Valuable clues to a bombing crime can be found in the piles of charred rubble and debris, but there is a human side to a crime scene, too. The victims who survive a blast are removed immediately from the scene so they can get medical help for their injuries. But the dead are also a part of the scene, and identifying all of them is of critical importance to investigators.

Why Identification Matters

Identification is important for many reasons. The most obvious, of course, is to give the victims' families and friends peace of mind. "It's really important to know one way or another," says one police officer. "In cases like Oklahoma City, or September 11, when lots of people are killed, the parents or spouses who have reason to believe their loved one might have been there—they are sick with worry. And even though the news is bad, it's better than not knowing. It lets people have a funeral, bury the body, whatever—and deal with the loss."[19]

Aside from easing the worry of the victims' friends and families, however, there are legal and economic reasons for identifying the bodies of the victims. A life insurance payment, for example, cannot be made until a person is declared legally dead, nor can an estate be settled if the status of the person involved is unknown. Death has to be certain before a marriage or business partnership can be dissolved, as well.

A final reason for identifying the victims is probably the most important to investigators. "Simply put," says one explosive expert, "it may be that among those who were killed by

A mourner visits the memorial to those killed in the bombing of the Alfred P. Murrah Federal Building in Oklahoma City.

the blast, the bomber himself could be there. Suicide bombers are not a rarity anymore, and that has to be carefully considered by the investigators at the scene."[20]

Early Examinations

The dead remain at the scene until their bodies are photographed and their location marked on a grid, just as pieces of evidence are. Forensic examiners X-ray every body and every part of a body, looking for tiny bits of the bomb's timer, detonator, or even the fragments of the container.

In Oklahoma City, for example, a great deal of evidence—including the same blue plastic fragments found at the scene—was recovered from the victims. Explains FBI investigator Danny Coulson, "When the blast went off, tens of thousands of slivers from the Ryder truck and the blue and white plastic drums that held the explosive charge screamed through the air, embedding in whatever they encountered. Many human bodies were shredded by these deadly projectiles."[21]

Besides being X-rayed, the bodies are swabbed for residue from the explosive. Examiners search through the victim's pockets, looking for any identification. In addition, they do fingertip searches, carefully feeling for any fragments that have lodged in the victim's clothing. Any burn marks on the body are noted, too. These may help investigators locate the seat of the explosion, if that has not already been determined.

"There Still Could Be Bodies Underneath the Train"

The proces of identifying the dead is often agonizingly slow. Sometimes this is because the bodies are difficult to retrieve. After the bombing of Pan Am 103 firefighters using hook and ladder trucks drove up and down a main street of Lockerbie looking for bodies on roofs or in the tops of trees. In other bombing scenes bodies lay hidden for days—or even weeks—buried under tons of rubble. The body of Wilfredo Mercado,

Developing a Latent Print on Paper

1 **Wearing protective gloves,** a technician takes the paper believed to have latent fingerprints on it and spreads it on a flat surface.

2 **The technician sprays** the paper with a thin mist of ninhydrin, which will react with the oils from the fingerprint.

3 **The paper** is placed into a microwave set at a low temperature for several minutes. The heat speeds up the chemical reaction of the fingerprint oils and ninhydrin.

4 **When the paper** is removed, any latent prints will be visible, appearing purplish blue.

Latent fingerprints like this one can be valuable clues to those who investigate bombings.

a victim of the World Trade Center bombing, was not located until seventeen days after the explosion.

After the London bombings of July 2005, in which terrorists set off explosives in three subway cars as well as a double-decker bus, bomb crews were frustrated in their investigation. Because of the cramped crime scene in the tunnel between King's Cross and Russell Square stations where one of the bombs had exploded, it was extremely difficult to remove the bodies. That particular tunnel is one of the deepest in London—more than 70 feet (21.34m) underground. Crews found that there were only a few inches of space between the ruined train and the tunnel walls.

Because of the cramped quarters only a few members of the crew could work at one time, retrieving body parts and swabbing them for evidence. Though they were certain there were no survivors among the bodies in the tunnel, investigators were unsure of the number of dead even four days after the blast. One speculated that some victims might have been blown out the front of the train and then run over as it skidded to a halt. "We have taken out all the bodies we can see," explained one deputy chief of the British Transport police, "but given that the blast was downward as well as sideways, there still could be bodies underneath the train."[22]

In some bombing scenes the slow pace can result in other concerns. In the tunnel near King's Cross, rats were a constant threat as they tried to carry off body parts. The site at Oklahoma City had similar problems. Because of the damage to the Murrah building, the piles of debris, which included body parts, clothing, and other material, was moved to a less populated area. It took examiners more than a week to go through the debris, and investigators acknowledge that predators were a source of concern during that time.

The cramped subway tunnels made searching for victims of the London transit bombings in July 2005 extremely difficult.

A Likely Bombing Suspect

In some cases the kind of damage done to the bodies at the scene can give investigators an idea of whether the bomber was killed in the blast. Someone carrying a bomb—either in a pack, or strapped to his or her chest as suicide bombers in the Middle East often do—suffers a great amount of damage to the skin and organs within the torso. The bomber's head and arms are often blown off, but these extremities usually lack gashes or other wounds. People near the bomber may also lose arms and legs in the explosion, but there are noticeable burns and other kinds of damage to those limbs.

The condition of one of the bodies in the London bombings was an important lead for investigators in July 2005. The bus that was bombed contained the remains of a body with the head ripped cleanly off. From identification found on the man's

Investigators searching the wreckage of this London bus found one body with its head ripped cleanly off, evidence that the attack was the work of a suicide bomber.

clothing, police were able to find out his name—Hasib Hussain. Hussain's mother had already reported her son missing, and after she provided a description of him, investigators realized they had a match. While the condition of the man's body was not irrefutable proof that he was the bomber, it gave detectives a lead to follow.

By the Numbers

$2.07 MILLION

Amount of financial damage caused by bombings in the United States in 2004

Fingerprints to Identify the Dead

Once the victims' bodies have been examined for evidence, medical examiners can begin the process of identifying them. There are a number of techniques by which bodies can be identified, and in a bombing investigation no one way is best. Everything depends on the condition of the body.

For many years the quickest, most legally binding identification technique has been fingerprinting. Everyone has a pattern of tiny ridges, or raised skin, on his or her fingertips. Visible with a magnifying glass, the ridges may be made up of whorls, or circles; arches, or horizontal ridges; and loops, or backward-curving ridges. No two people have the same fingerprints, not even identical twins. That means that if a fingerprint obtained from a victim's body matches a sample of that person's fingerprints provided by the family, for example, the examiner can say with certainty the identity of that body.

"A lot of people would say, 'I don't have any prints of my husband, or child,' or whatever," says Amy, a lab technician.

> They are thinking an inked print, like the ones provided by people being booked at the police station. And right, few of us would have a document with the inked prints of our family members. That would be really helpful to police, but extremely unlikely.

What police use in victim identification is a latent print. A latent print is different from one you could easily see. A print left by someone with blood on their hands would not be latent. But the ridges of the fingerprint have oils, salts, and other residue that can leave a mark on a letter, a glass, on any number of things, no matter how clean the person's hands were. And that fingerprint can be developed in the lab, so that it is as easy to read as a bloody one.[23]

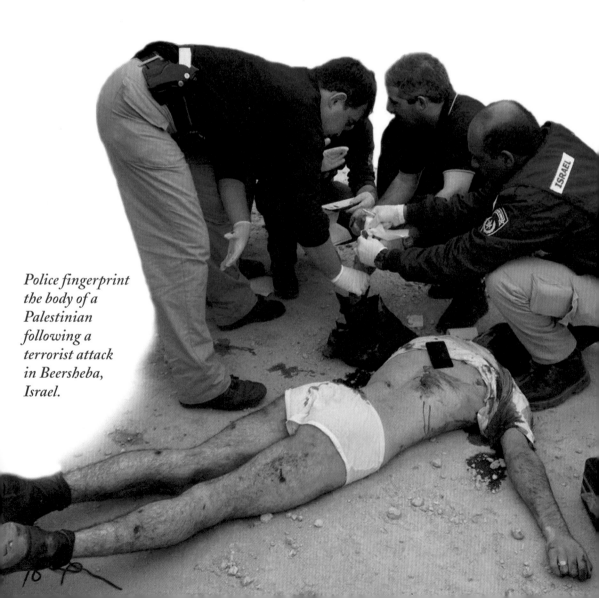

Police fingerprint the body of a Palestinian following a terrorist attack in Beersheba, Israel.

Fingerprinting the Dead

After the London bombing, police officers visited the homes of victims of the blasts to gather any household objects likely to have a latent print. These objects were then processed in the lab and compared to inked prints obtained from the victims. About a dozen of the fifty-five victims of the bombing were identified by such comparisons.

Sometimes, however, getting clear fingerprints from a dead body is extremely difficult. It is common for skin—including the skin on the fingertips—to be damaged or burned in an explosion, and as a result the thin ridges that make up the print seem to be unreadable. When this happens forensic pathologists can use more unusual techniques of obtaining fingerprints.

One such technique is to inject a saline solution called tissue builder into the fingertip. Tissue builder causes the fingertips to swell to a more normal shape so they can be fingerprinted. In other cases the epidermis, or outer layer of skin, may be so burned that the ridges cannot be seen at all. Pathologists can cut the epidermis away and the ridges can be obtained from the second layer of skin. In severe cases where the second layer of skin is intact but is too soft or flabby to be fingerprinted, the pathologist may cut the skin off, slide it on his or her own finger, and print it that way.

Using DNA to Identify Victims

If the body is too damaged for fingerprinting to be an option, investigators rely on DNA samples. DNA is located in the nucleus of the body's cells, and scientists have learned that its long strands contain information that is unique to each individual—although DNA does not differ in identical twins, as fingerprints do.

When scientists learned how to separate DNA from the matter in which it is found, such as blood, hair, skin, and so on, they began to create DNA "fingerprints" or profiles. These DNA fingerprints have been used with increasing frequency in criminal cases where a perpetrator's blood, skin, or other cells have been left at a crime scene. By matching that evidence with a sample of a suspect's DNA, detectives have been able to prove the suspect was present at that crime scene.

DNA is even more useful in identifying victims, such as those of an explosion. "With a criminal case, like a rape or murder, you can have a sample of DNA, but unless you have a suspect to compare it to, it's useless," says Amy.

There are computer databases of DNA, but they are primarily made up of offenders. In the case of a catastrophe, like a fire or a bombing, where investigators

Becoming a Forensic Chemist

Job Description:
A forensic chemist is responsible for isolating and identifying chemicals—including explosives—found at a crime scene.

Education:
A bachelor's degree in biology, physics, or chemistry is required. In addition, a forensic chemist needs several semesters of higher mathematics, especially calculus.

Qualifications:
A thorough knowledge of the use of the gas chromatograph/mass spectrometer, the high performance liquid chromatograph (HPLC), and other instruments is required. In addition the forensic chemist must be able to analyze and identify trace elements of chemical mixtures and write reports to investigators on what has been found. In many cases, the forensic chemist may need to be able to explain his or her findings in court.

Salary:
A starting salary for an inexperienced forensic chemist ranges from $30,000 to $33,000.

find out pretty quickly who the likely victims were, it becomes a process of matching the samples taken from the bodies to samples provided by family members. You're not talking about an unknown perpetrator.[24]

Creating an Autorad

Just as London police gathered objects likely to have fingerprints of the victims, they requested family members to supply them with sources of DNA. This genetic material can be found in many places—from hair in a hairbrush to saliva or skin cells on the bristles of the victim's toothbrush. Whatever seems a likely source is brought into the lab, where technicians use certain chemicals to separate the DNA from the material in which it was found. The DNA strands are tightly coiled inside the nucleus of each cell, but if unrolled they would be about 6 feet (1.8m) long.

Not all of the strand is of interest to the forensic technicians, however. Scientists have found that most of the hereditary information contained in the strand is common to all humans. Only very small sections, called polymorphisms, have information that will help identify a particular person. A scientist uses a special chemical to cut the DNA strand into small fragment lengths so that the polymorphisms can be analyzed.

By attaching a radioactive molecule to the polymorphisms, scientists can make an X-ray of them. This X-ray, called an autorad, looks like a blurry bar code found on products in a grocery store. The victim's autorad can be compared to the autorad of a sample provided by the family.

Autorads like this, made from DNA from a bombing victim, can be compared to an autorad created from DNA from a known source, such as hair from a brush, to confirm identity.

47

Teeth and Pacemakers

In many bombing cases the use of dental records can help identify victims, too. In the Pan Am 103 bombing, some of the victims were burned beyond recognition, making fingerprinting extremely difficult. Obtaining and organizing DNA samples from family members in the United States would not have been feasible in 1988, since there was not yet an organization in place that could handle such a large-scale DNA project. Dental identification, therefore, proved very helpful.

The Bomb That Killed No One

The most sophisticated bomb ever planted in the United States was a 3,000-pound (1,360kg) device that looked more like a washing machine than a bomb. The bombers, disguised as workmen, wheeled it into Harvey's Wagon Wheel Resort in Lake Tahoe, Nevada, on August 29, 1980. It had a note attached, warning that any attempt to disarm the bomb would be unsuccessful.

The large resort evacuated all guests and workers, and explosives experts assessed the device and realized that it was the most complex bomb they had ever seen. "This was quite a bomb," recalls one investigator, quoted in David Fisher's *Hard Evidence*. "It had 28 toggle switches and it was designed so that if two specific switches were put in the correct position it could be moved. Supposedly when the $3 million ransom was paid, the bomb makers would tell us which two switches would make it safe."

The bomb squad attempted to disarm the bomb by remote control, but they were unsuccessful. More than 1,000 pounds (453kg) of dynamite blew out the inside of the resort, resulting in a five-story cavity in the building. Remarkably, no one was killed. Authorities eventually caught the bombers, who were arrested and sent to prison.

Unlike skin, teeth almost always survive an explosion or fire. Forensic examiners usually take dental X-rays of the victim. They carefully chart all fillings, crowns, root canals, and any unusual spacing between teeth. Once the victim's teeth have been charted, examiners compare the chart to dental records provided by the family of the likely victim.

Another means of identification, though only useful in certain cases, is that of surgical devices. Since 1993 doctors have been required by law to record the serial number of any surgical hardware they install on a patient's body—from pacemakers to artificial hips and breast implants. Medical examiners can track the device's serial number on a computer database and quickly find out the name of the recipient.

No one identification method will work with bombing victims whose bodies have suffered so much trauma. And in cases where the retrieval of bodies and body parts has been exceptionally difficult, the process can be excruciatingly long for family members waiting for news of a loved one. Ian Blair, the commissioner of Scotland Yard who headed the London bombing investigation, apologized for the slow pace but insisted that it was necessary to be painstakingly careful. "I appeal to everybody to give us time," he said at a news conference just a few days after the bombings. "We have got to get this right."[25]

Forensic experts would agree. Whatever method they use to get a positive identification—a fingerprint, a DNA sample, or some other means—their mission is crucial, and accuracy is paramount. Being able to change a generic label of Jane Doe or John Doe to the victim's real name is a small but very important victory.

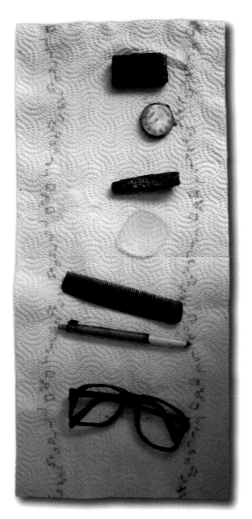

Personal items can serve as clues to the identity of bombing victims.

CHAPTER 4

Working with the Evidence

O nce all debris and other material of interest has been collected and removed from the site of a bombing, investigators begin the process of sifting through it. The hope, of course, is to find any evidence that might lead them to the bombers. Apart from finding a part of the bomber's vehicle, as they did in Oklahoma City and the World Trade Center, investigators consider the location of any part of the bomb or explosive the most promising lead in identifying those responsible.

Testing the Cotton Swabs

At the forensic laboratory, technicians remove the cotton balls that have been used to swab the doors, walls, and even the skin of the victims for explosives residue. If technicians suspect that the substance on the swabs is gunpowder, they may look at a portion of the material under a microscope to be certain. On the other hand, if a more sophisticated explosive, such as Semtex, is suspected, technicians use a very sensitive instrument called a high performance liquid chromatograph, or HPLC. It is so sensitive, in fact, that it can detect a few nanograms of explosive in a sample. (A nanogram is 1,000 millionths of a gram.)

First, residue from the cotton ball is fed into the HPLC, where it is propelled through a long, thin tube. Each compound in the sample progresses through the tube at a different rate, depending on its chemical makeup. A computer attached to the HPLC identifies the rate of speed of each compound. Based on its rate of speed, a second instrument can identify the compound, thereby giving investigators the exact makeup of the explosive used in the bomb.

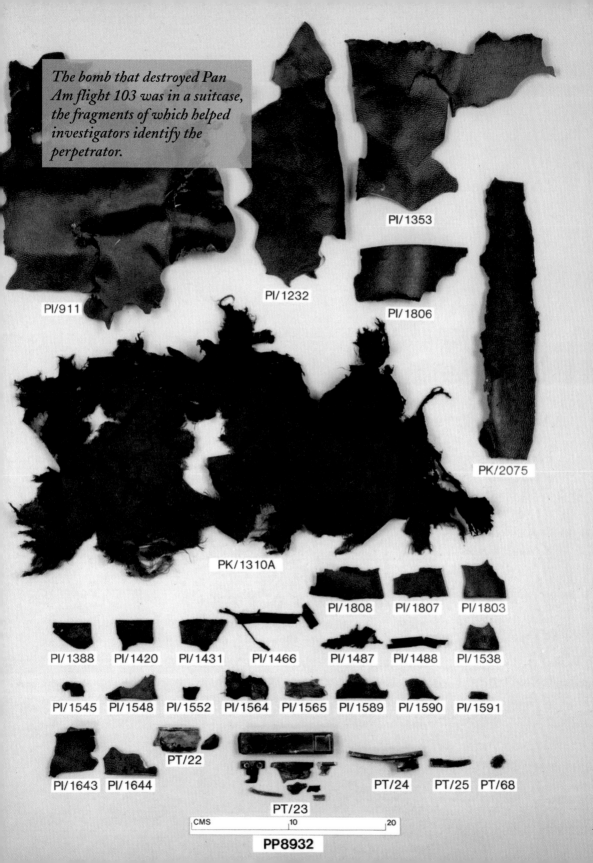

The bomb that destroyed Pan Am flight 103 was in a suitcase, the fragments of which helped investigators identify the perpetrator.

PI/1353

PI/911

PI/1232

PI/1806

PK/2075

PK/1310A

PI/1808   PI/1807   PI/1803

PI/1388   PI/1420   PI/1431   PI/1466   PI/1487   PI/1488   PI/1538

PI/1545   PI/1548   PI/1552   PI/1564   PI/1565   PI/1589   PI/1590   PI/1591

PT/22

PI/1643   PI/1644

PT/24   PT/25   PT/68

PT/23

CMS   10   20

PP8932

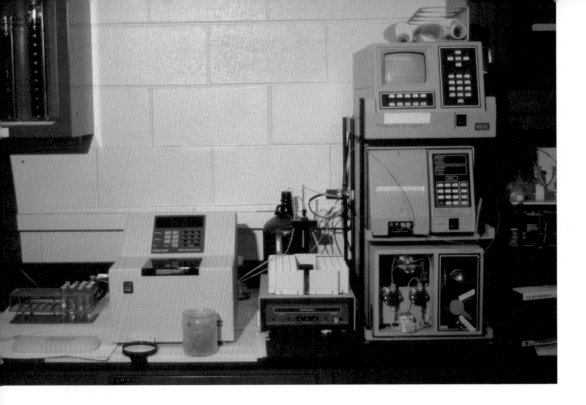

An extremely sensitive instrument known as an HPLC can detect residues from the sophisticated explosives used by many terrorists.

When fragments of the Pan Am airplane were swabbed at a London forensic laboratory, technicians verified that the explosive in the bomb was Semtex. This was important information for investigators. Since Semtex was almost always associated with terrorist bombings, its residue pointed to an act of terrorism rather than a bomb set to murder of one of the passengers. After that finding, investigators turned their sights almost exclusively to terrorist groups.

"The Mother of Satan"

In the London bombings, swabs confirmed that a different explosive known as TATP, short for triacetone triperoxide, was one of the bomb components. TATP has been used by many terrorists, including a great number of suicide attackers in Israel as well as by operatives of al Qaeda, the terrorist group led by Osama bin Laden that took responsibility for attacks in the United States on September 11, 2001. The use of TATP indicated to London investigators that there was a good chance that the bombers were extremist Muslims—perhaps part of al Qaeda.

Osama bin Laden leads the terrorist group al Qaeda, which is believed to be responsible for the London transit bombings.

Experts say that TATP can be concocted from a variety of ingredients, such as drain cleaner and bleach, that can be easily purchased without raising suspicion. It is also a very powerful homemade explosive—so unstable and so often accidentally detonated that forty Palestinian terrorists are known to have been killed handling it. It is not hard to understand why TATP is often called the "Mother of Satan." When he learned that TATP was found in the residue of the blasts, one British explosives expert noted, "Frankly, I wouldn't want to be wandering around with ten pounds of TATP on my back."[26]

Rebuilding a Plane

In the Pan Am 103 case, knowing the type of explosive used was helpful, but investigators needed to know more about how it got on the plane. Was it brought aboard by a suicide bomber, or was one of the passengers carrying the device unknowingly? To help answer this question it was necessary to know where the bomb was when it exploded.

In the days after the crash, searchers located two pieces of metal from the airplane that were identified as part of the luggage container. Once the lab found that there was a great deal of explosives residue on the pieces, experts deduced that the bomb must have been very close to those pieces when it exploded. "What was so important about it," says Tom Thurman, an explosives expert at the FBI, "was that it told us that the bomb had been in the baggage area rather than in the passenger cabin."[27]

But there was no way of knowing which baggage area on the large airplane the bomb had been in. To find that out, investigators decided to try to rebuild the craft from the fragments that had been found in Scotland and see if they could ascertain the exact point of the explosion. Unbelievably, about 4 million pieces of the wreckage—some of them less than an inch (2.54cm) across—had been found by search crews. The fragments that were believed to be part of the airplane were taken to a hangar at a British air force base west of London, and the gigantic reconstruction project began.

"It Was, Quite Simply, a Jigsaw Puzzle"

Crews used a full-size wire frame as a base and began to assemble the airliner three weeks after the bombing. Technicians from Britain's Air Accident Investigations Board (AAIB) assisted the crews, helping them find the exact spot on the frame for each of the fragments that had been found.

A Tiny Piece of a Bomb's Timer

Though forensic crews and investigators searched for months and found millions of pieces of the airplane and its luggage, only one piece of the bomb that destroyed Pan Am 103 was ever found. A man walking his dog in the Scottish countryside found a scrap of a shirt from the blast. Looking at it carefully, examiners noticed that there was a tiny piece of a green circuit board embedded in the material.

Investigators learned that it was actually a piece of the bomb's timing mechanism. Under a microscope, forensic examiners were able to make out parts of letters on the board and subsequently traced it to a Swiss company known for its expensive high-quality

Scottish investigators search the area around the cockpit of Pan Am flight 103.

timers. Officials at the firm supplied their customer lists that showed that a Libyan official had purchased twenty such timers. This evidence supported the idea that Libyan terrorists were involved in the bombing.

One Scottish police officer visited the hangar during the process and was amazed at what he saw. "They literally put the nose at one end and [pieces of] the tail at the other," he later said, "and started assembling the pieces in between. It was, quite simply, a jigsaw puzzle."[28]

A little over 90 percent of the structure had been recovered, but even though sections on the wire frame were missing, there was enough of the plane for investigators to see what they were hoping to see. "As more and more pieces [of the plane] were hung," recalls a lead investigator of the bombing, "we started seeing some abnormal bending and crunching of the metal around the baggage area. Then, about seven hundred inches [1,778cm] back on the left side of the aircraft, we could see soot and residue, and finally, there was a big hole."[29]

By seeing exactly which luggage container had been the one in which the bomb was placed, investigators were able to search airline passenger records and learn that a suitcase in that particular spot had been checked by a passenger who did not show up for the flight. That information told investigators that the blast was not caused by a suicide bomber.

Investigators reassembled the Pan Am jetliner destroyed over Lockerbie, Scotland, in their effort to discover who was behind the bombing.

In the process of assembling the plane, crews found another interesting piece of evidence. In the wall of the luggage
container where the bomb had been were three tiny pieces of
gray plastic that appeared to be the sort of material used in
electronics equipment. They also found fragments of a cop-
per-colored suitcase that had clearly been damaged by the explosive. Because both sets of fragments had suffered the same
type of damage, investigators were certain that they were linked
to the bomber somehow.

Forensic lab technicians looked at the gray plastic fragments under a microscope and learned from the tiny numbers and other details on them that they were part of a Toshiba
radio-cassette player. They examined the suitcase fragments
and found that the material was consistent with a style made
by Samsonite.

These finds told investigators that the bomb had been hidden inside the Toshiba radio-cassette player, which was placed
in a Samsonite suitcase that was later loaded onto the plane.
From the damage to the plane, they could see that the suitcase
had been placed in the left side baggage compartment, right under the big blue P of the Pan American logo painted on the plane.

These were not answers, but the information provided new
leads for the investigation. Perhaps investigators could locate
all purchasers of that model of Toshiba radio-cassette player
or of that particular style of Samsonite luggage. Although it
was a formidable task—since both brands were highly popular around the world—investigators were pleased that they
knew more than they had previously.

The "Fingerprint" of a Tool Mark

Sometimes it is a mark or scratch on a bomb fragment or other piece of evidence that provides new information for investigators. Experts say that important clues can sometimes be
found in the marks used by the bomber's tools—screwdrivers,
bolt cutters, knives, pliers, and so on. Common tools may all
look the same, but under a microscope they are very different.

Every blade or edge has minute imperfections that make it easily identifiable to a trained forensic scientist. Some of these imperfections originate in the tool's manufacture, while others occur because of wear and tear. No matter what their source, the gouges, nicks, or scratches on the blade of a tool can sometimes be seen on bomb fragments.

The forensic scientist checks any marks left by the tool on a fragment and notes the imperfections. Of course, that information is helpful only if investigators have a suspect in the bombing. If they do, they search the suspect's home, garage, and vehicles for any tools that might have made those particular marks.

In the lab the suspect's tool is used to make a mark in some soft surface, such as clay or putty. This ensures that the blade is not damaged more during the laboratory test, thus making the results questionable. After making a mark with the tool, a technician uses a special microscope that can look at both marks side by side—the sample and the one from the bomb fragment. By viewing the original toolmark side by side with the test sample, the technician can say with a high degree of certainty if the marks were made with the same tool.

A Pipe Bomb at K-Mart

The imperfections on the blade of a knife helped solve a bombing that occurred in Indianapolis, Indiana, in 1989. A five-year-old girl named Erin Bower was with her family shopping at K-Mart. On a shelf loaded with a display of toothpaste there was an unusual container, and Erin reached for it. "I looked inside and there were wires," she recalled years later, "and I knew something was wrong. Then I set it down and that's when it blew up."[30] The container was actually a pipe bomb that was loaded with BBs as shrapnel. It blew off Erin's hand, and the fragments set her clothes on fire, causing severe burns. Her left eye was so damaged that doctors were forced to remove it.

No one had any idea who had placed a bomb in the store until a day later, when David Swinford, a local high school

Becoming a Tool Mark Examiner

Job Description:
A tool mark examiner analyzes markings on evidence that are likely to have been made by the perpetrator of a crime using some sort of tool. The examiner forms conclusions based on tests with the evidence, prepares written reports, and may be called on to testify as an expert witness in court cases.

Tool mark examiners are often called upon to testify about their findings in court.

Education:
A four-year college degree in physical science, chemistry, physics, criminalistics, or a related field is usually required. Most employers require at least a year of working in a laboratory under the supervision of a veteran examiner.

Qualifications:
A tool mark examiner must have experience in laboratory testing methods, the use of microscopes needed to analyze tool marks, and must be aware of any and all regulations concerning the handling and storage of criminal evidence. The examiner must also be a good communicator, both orally and in writing.

Salary:
$50,000–$60,000.

senior, committed suicide. His family told bombing investigators that they suspected he might have set the bomb and afterward killed himself when he realized the suffering he had caused. To know for certain, however, investigators needed to find evidence that would verify the family's suspicions.

Forensic examiners immediately noted that there were unusual marks on the container's plastic cap and examined them under the microscope. They surmised that the bomber had used a knife with a damaged blade to cut a hole for the switch on the bomb. Investigators searched Swinford's car and found such a damaged knife. After conducting tests on the tool, they found the marks from it matched those on the plastic cap, thus allowing investigators to close the case.

An Unusual Bomb and a Stalled Investigation

Sometimes a promising lead can come not only from examining the evidence in the lab but from remembering the details of a previous bombing case. For example, after Judge Robert Vance and attorney Robert Robinson were each killed by pipe bombs that came to them through the mail in December 1989, FBI investigators followed standard procedure—identifying the components of the bomb and the explosive used. However, the investigation stalled when none of the components were traceable to any individual.

All that changed because of a breakfast meeting at a restaurant near Atlanta, Georgia. Called the Metro Bomb Meeting, it was an informal monthly gathering of a dozen state, local, and federal bomb experts who shared stories about current and past cases and discussed interesting new developments in forensic technology.

During a meeting held soon after the letter bomb murders, the FBI agent working on the case described to his associates the pipe bomb the killer had used. It was unusual, he said, because the bomber had capped the pipe on both ends with square

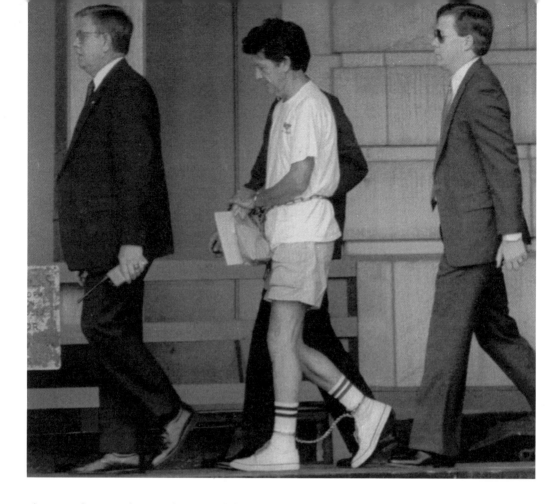

plates and painted everything with black enamel paint. But even though the bomb was far different from other pipe bombs agents had seen, he said, the investigation was going nowhere.

The unusual bomb construction methods of Walter Leroy Moody, shown here being escorted into court, were an important clue to his identity.

A Bomber's Signature

One of the men at the meeting, an ATF forensic expert named Lloyd Erwin, was keenly interested in the description of the letter bombs, for he had seen a very similar bomb seventeen years before. The square end plates of the bomb and the black enamel paint were so unusual that he remembered them vividly. In the case Erwin had worked on, a young woman had been injured by the letter bomb, and the bomber—a man named Walter Leroy Moody—had been caught and convicted. "He's bound to be out," Erwin told the agent. "That's been a long time ago, the way they let people out of prison nowadays."[31]

The unusual construction of those bombs is referred to as the bomber's "signature." Moody was a creature of habit in building his bombs, as are many other bombers. He had his own style, which included using the same type and quantity of explosive and painting each of his bombs black. Experts say that two bombers could use the same components and yet their finished products would almost always differ in subtle ways. "People learn to make bombs one way," says one explosives expert, "and no matter how sophisticated they get, they'll continue to repeat certain techniques. That technique is almost as unique as a fingerprint, and it makes strong evidence that two or more bombs were made by the same person or group."[32]

Terrorists from al Qaeda used a series of bombs to destroy three trains in Madrid, Spain, killing 191 people and injuring more than 1,500 others.

In this case Erwin's accurate memory changed the whole investigation. By turning their attention to Moody as a suspect, investigators were able to build a strong case. Moody was eventually convicted of the bombing murders and sentenced to seven life terms in prison.

Today's investigators do not need to rely on their memory of bombing details from years past. The ATF maintains a database called BATS (Bombing Arson Tracking System),

States with the Most Bombing Incidents in 2004

Washington 54
California 210
Arizona 54
Texas 88
Missouri 60
Illinois 53
Kentucky 45
Tennessee 138
Pennsylvania 68
Florida 71

Total: 841

Source: Bureau of Alcohol, Tobacco, Firearms and Explosives

which contains and sorts every detail from virtually every bombing incident that occurs in the United States. An investigator can search it for certain specifics about other cases—type of explosive, method of detonation, and so on. If another case has had similar characteristics, that may provide new angles for investigators to explore.

A Lucky Find

For a bombing investigation, just as fortunate as a colleague recognizing a bomber's signature is finding an unexploded bomb. As FBI expert David Fisher says, "For investigators, getting a bomb intact is like finding the Holy Grail, only more valuable."[33] The reason is that the device is whole and as the bomb maker created it, rather than blown into tiny fragments that must be reconstructed before investigators can really examine it for clues. Though it is a rare occurence, an unexploded bomb can prove priceless to an investigation such as the one that took place after the bombings in Madrid in March 2004.

A series of ten bombs were exploded on four different trains during morning rush hour, killing 191 people and wounding more than 1,500 others. As investigators scrambled to gather evidence, many government officials in Spain believed that the bombers were most likely members of the terrorist organization Euskadi Ta Askatasuna (ETA), a group that had long demanded the creation of a separate state in parts of northern Spain. However, the discovery of an unexploded bomb turned the investigation around.

The bomb was found by a rescue worker who had been looking for survivors in the wreckage of the trains. He found a sports bag that he believed to be luggage belonging to one of the victims. It was taken to a local police station and added to a large pile of unclaimed bags, purses, luggage, and other personal effects. Twelve hours after the bombing an alarm sounded from inside the spots bag. When detectives looked inside, they found a bomb made of 22 pounds (9.97kg) of dynamite, with screws and nails as shrapnel.

A SIM Card Leads to Arrests

Attached to the explosive was a cell phone with its alarm buzzing. No one knows why the bomb did not explode, but it gave investigators a new lead. The phone, when called by the bomber's phone, would have completed a circuit within the bomb and ignited it.

If the bomb had gone off, of course, the cell phone would have been destroyed. But technicians were able to get two sorts of evidence from the unexploded device. The first was the Subscriber Identity Module, or SIM card, a chip embedded in every cell phone that contains not only the personal phone book for that phone but also the name and address of the owner. The second was a clear fingerprint.

These clues led to seventeen arrests—not of ETA members but of radical Islamists operating an al Qaeda cell in Spain. As it turned out, the unexploded device, one investigator noted, "was a gift that gave [police] the necessary help to find people responsible for such a barbaric act."[34]

CHAPTER 5

Watchful Eyes

A bombing investigation is not necessarily limited to evidence processed in the forensic laboratory. Sometimes a witness may provide important clues such as a description of a suspect or a vehicle's license plate number. Other times the lab evidence itself may lead investigators to people who have come in contact with the bomber. Either way, investigators know that speaking with people who may have seen the suspect can help them move closer to an arrest.

"He Was Standing Right Next to Me"

After the London bombings on July 7, 2005, a man came forward with information that he felt might help the police. Richard Jones, a sixty-one-year-old businessman, had been a passenger on the Number 30 double-decker bus that was bombed. He told police that he had a good look at the bomber, whom he described as a young, handsome, olive-skinned man who had a knapsack with him. He told police that the man seemed agitated about something.

"He was standing next to me with the bag at his feet, and he kept dipping into this bag and fiddling about with something," Jones told police. "I was getting quite annoyed, because this was a crowded bus. You can imagine the crush—it was standing room only. Everybody is standing face to face, and this guy kept dipping into his bag."[35]

Jones said that he became irritated that the bus was moving so slowly and got off before his normal stop—a decision that likely saved him from death or injury in that blast, which killed thirteen of the passengers.

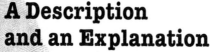

A Description and an Explanation

Hasib Hussain is believed to be one of the suicide bombers involved in the attacks on the London transit system in July 2005.

Another witness who noticed the bus idling in a London square agreed that it had been moving slowly. After the second of the four blasts, which had occurred nearly an hour before on the subway, traffic had been rerouted to make way for emergency vehicles. The bus driver, said the witness, seemed confused about how to get to his passengers' destinations and asked directions from a police officer. Moments later the bomb exploded.

The witnesses' accounts helped investigators in two ways. First, Jones's description of the man with the knapsack matched the victim who was beheaded by the blast and whom police believed was the bomber. He was eighteen-year-old Hasib Hussain, whose family had called police because he was missing.

The information about the slow bus and the confused driver provided an explanation about what the man was doing with this knapsack. "We now assume he was adjusting a timer or something on the bomb itself," explained one investigator to news reporters. "He was nervous about it, according to witnesses, maybe because it was set to go off at a later point, and since there were delays . . . the timing was off, or something. We can only speculate now, but that seems a likely explanation."[36]

"As Good a Witness as We Could Have Hoped For"

Witnesses were also key to the arrest of those responsible for the Oklahoma City bombing. The initial finding of the VIN number on the truck's axle in the ruins

of the Murrah Federal Building allowed agents to track down the rental agency in Junction City, Kansas, that leased the vehicle.

The agents who went to the rental office hoped to get at least a partial description of the person who rented the van, although investigators are aware that when such offices are busy, clerks often do not have time to notice what a customer looks like. However, they were pleasantly surprised when they talked to the manager of the officer, Eldon Elliott. Coulson, the investigator who visited Junction City, says that Elliott remembered the man well.

"Eldon Elliott, it turned out, was as good a witness as we could have hoped for," Coulson recalls. "He got a good look at [the man]. He was a white male, about his own height, five

feet ten, twenty-seven to thirty, average build, military style haircut, no facial hair, no accent. Elliott said it was possible the man had worn camouflage-colored clothing."[37]

Using a Sketch Artist

Coulson and his fellow agents were disappointed, but not surprised, that the information on the rental agreement—name, address, and so on—was made up. The name given was Robert Kling, and extensive checking showed that there was no such resident at the address given, nor could they find a Robert Kling that matched the description given by Elliott.

They decided to have Elliott work with an FBI sketch artist to develop a likeness of the renter. When Elliott was satisfied with the results, thousands of federal, state, and local law enforcement agents began to circulate copies of the sketch on a likely route between Junction City and Oklahoma City. The owner of the Dreamland Motel in Junction City recognized the face right away as that of a man who had stayed in the motel. She produced the sign-in records, and the name on the register was Tim McVeigh.

This sketch shows a suspected conspirator in the Oklahoma City bombing who has never been identified or caught.

The value of the sketch was crucial, for once investigators were able to get the name of the suspect, they found out more about Timothy McVeigh that pointed to his involvement in the bombing. Another witness, a former army friend of McVeigh's named Michael Fortier, admitted to detectives that he knew that his friend was planning to bomb the building. "He . . . told me that he had figured out how to make a truck into a bomb," Fortier said. "He explained to me how he would arrange the barrels, five-gallon drums in the back of that truck."[38]

A Baby's Sleeper

Evidence also led investigators to helpful witnesses in the Pan Am 103 bombing. More than six months after the bombing, some detectives were still combing the Scottish countryside looking for debris that would help them identify a suspect in the case. They found a scrap of blue cotton cloth that, upon careful examination, proved to be part of a sleeper, a garment for a very small baby.

Forensic examiners were excited by the find because, unlike other clothing gathered on the ground, this piece of cloth was scorched. Tests on the fabric showed traces of Semtex, the explosive used in the bomb, so the sleeper had definitely been inside the Samsonite suitcase containing the bomb.

Even more exciting for investigators, the label on the scrap was intact. The manufacturer was Babygro, and detectives found that the sleeper was made and sold only in Malta, an island country in the Mediterranean Sea. Calls to the manufacturer revealed that the blue sleeper was one of a small batch that was sold at a store called Mary's House in Sliema, Malta.

Identifying a Suspect

When they visited Mary's House, investigators were surprised to learn that the shopkeeper remembered selling a blue Babygro sleeper to a man not too long before the bombing of Pan Am 103. The shopkeeper's memory of the sale was vivid, he said, because the man had bought a lot of unrelated clothing and seemed not to care what size or color of clothing he was buying. "He remembered one pair of pants in particular," says one of the investigators, "because they were so ugly."[39] The witness was able to describe the

Federal investigators circulated this sketch of a suspect in the Oklahoma City bombing, and soon learned from a witness that his name was Timothy McVeigh.

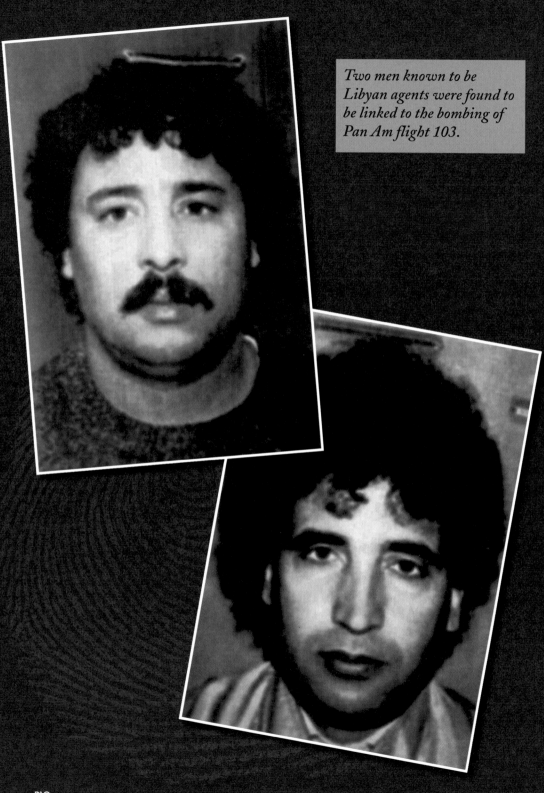

Two men known to be Libyan agents were found to be linked to the bombing of Pan Am flight 103.

customer as a clean-shaven man in his thirties, who spoke with a Libyan accent.

As a result of interviewing this witness, detectives verified their suspicions that one or more Libyan terrorists were involved. Relying heavily on local law enforcement, they concentrated on Libyan people with terrorist connections in Malta and created a photo array—a collection of photographs of men who generally fit the shopkeeper's description.

They presented the array to the shopkeeper, and he picked out the photograph of Abdel Basset Ali Al-Magrahi, a Libyan intelligence agent who had been suspected of terrorist activity. "That interview was an important piece of the investigation," says one investigator who followed the case. "The astronomical chances against that piece of cloth surviving the explosion, and the ability of the witness at Mary's House—it came together to give them a viable suspect."[40]

The Witnesses That Never Sleep

Some valuable descriptions of bombers come from nonhuman sources—namely, surveillance cameras. London, with half a million surveillance cameras placed throughout stores, public squares, and street corners, is probably the most heavily filmed city in the world. Experts estimate that the average Londoner appears on film from the closed circuit television system (CCTV) three hundred times daily.

The CCTV system has been valuable in solving at least two high-profile bombing incidents. The first was that of David Copeland, known as the Nail Bomber because he used long, razor-sharp nails as shrapnel. After his first bombing on April 17, 1999, which seriously injured twenty-eight people outside a London market, police were frustrated at the lack of witnesses or usable evidence. They began looking at footage from CCTV cameras in the area,

By the Numbers

4 MILLION

Number of CCTV cameras in Britain

hoping to catch a glimpse of someone leaving a suspicious bag outside the store.

Police viewed twenty-six hundred hours of footage from dozens of cameras. After three weeks, they found a shot of a figure leaving a bag in the doorway of the market. The image was grainy and the lighting poor, however—so much so that investigators were unable to tell even whether the figure was male or female.

Help from NASA

London bomb investigators turned to the National Aeronautics and Space Administration (NASA) in Houston, Texas, hoping that the agency's experience with enhancing satellite images from outer space could help detectives see the figure more clearly. The NASA computers ultimately provided an image of a man wearing a baseball cap, looking around the entrance of the market almost two hours before the explosion.

The enhanced photograph was released to the London media on April 29, 1999. Investigators asked the public for help in identifying the man—who by this time had bombed another market, seriously injuring thirteen people. Very shortly after the release of the photo, a coworker of David Copeland identified him. He was arrested and convicted of murder in June 2000.

"We're Working at It Day and Night"

After the David Copeland case, London's municipal government increased the number of its CCTV cameras and improved the quality of their images. When four bombs went off in London on July 7, 2005, police hoped the cameras would prove helpful once again.

One police spokesperson was so confident that they would find the bombers on camera that he promised an early conclusion to their investigation. "It took just three weeks to find David Copeland," he said, "I think police will identify these bombers in a similar time because the systems involved are

Cameras like this one mounted on a lamppost near the clock tower in Parliament Square proved vital in helping police determine who attacked the London transit system in July 2005.

The Shoe Bomber

One of the most famous cases in which an airline bombing was averted is that of Richard Reid, known as the Shoe Bomber. Reid was arrested on December 22, 2001, for attempting to blow up an American Airlines flight from Paris to Miami.

A flight attendant noticed that Reid was trying to light a match on the tongue of his tennis shoe. After she tried to grab his shoe from his hand, he pushed her to the floor and continued trying to ignite his shoe. Passengers subdued Reid until the plane landed. Investigators found that Reid's shoe contained plastic explosives and a TATP detonator—enough to blow up the plane.

Richard Reid attempted to set off explosives aboard an American Airlines flight bound from Paris to Miami.

Reid stated that he was an Islamic fundamentalist and was in league with al Qaeda, the terrorist organization headed by Osama bin Laden. On January 30, 2003, he was found guilty of terrorism and sentenced to life in prison.

much better. We should within two weeks at least have some image of the bombers."[41]

The task was far more daunting than that of the Nail Bomber, however, because there are six thousand cameras in the London Underground alone—not counting the more than eighteen hundred cameras in the train stations themselves. Besides all of those cameras, police recovered cameras outside each of the forty stations on the trains' routes, as well as cameras in the areas where passengers boarded the No. 30 bus. It was, according to police, the largest CCTV recovery the department had ever participated in. "It's a massive job that is very time consuming," noted one officer. "It sounds impossible."[42]

London police viewed thousands of hours of footage, and Scotland Yard deployed extra officers, bringing the number of viewers to fifteen hundred. "We are working at it day and night," one investigator explained. "Twenty-four hours, round the clock. We've no room for mistakes here, so everyone is very keyed in to their task."[43]

Success

The positive identification of Hussain as one of the bombers enabled investigators to look for his image. And because

Security cameras recorded the arrival at a railway station of the four men later identified as the suicide bombers who attacked the London transit system.

Hussain's family had provided pictures of some of his friends, police looked for their likenesses on the video, too. Four days after beginning the video search, police officers found what they were looking for.

In the footage taken at King's Cross railway station at 8:20 A.M., Hussain was laughing and talking with three other men.

Becoming a Special Agent with the ATF

Job Description:
A special agent investigates criminal violations of federal laws concerning explosives, firearms, arson, and other matters. An agent gathers and analyzes evidence through investigative leads, seizures, and arrests, and testifies for the government in court.

Education:
To be considered for this position, an applicant must have either a bachelor's degree, three years or more of experience in law enforcement, or a combination of college and criminal investigative experience.

Qualifications:
An ATF special agent must be in good physical shape, must be between the ages of twenty-one and thirty-seven for his or her first appointment, must take a polygraph (lie detector) test, and pass a background check to receive top secret clearance from the government. An agent must be willing to handle rigorous physical and mental training as well as extensive travel and personal risk on the job.

Salary:
The base salary for a special agent with no previous experience is $30,400 per year.

On June 28, 2005, security cameras in Luton, in central England, recorded these three men, later identified as suicide bombers, as they staged a dry run of their attack on the London transit system.

One officer viewing the film was stunned at how happy and relaxed the men looked, saying, "You'd think they were going on a hiking holiday."[44] The three talked for a minute or two, and then each went a different way. Twenty minutes later the first of the bombs went off.

With a better idea of the time frame of the men's arrival at King's Cross, police looked at additional video hoping to trace their previous movements. Fortunately for investigators, the men had been recorded waiting for a train at Luton station, about 30 miles (48km) north of London. The fact that they all came from one place helped police concentrate on a particular area. In the days that followed, investigators made raids at the homes of three of the bombers and gathered more information about them. The silent cameras of the CCTV system had proved a success once again.

CHAPTER 6

The Bomber's Own Words

Bombing cases are often solved because of evidence that is recovered from the scene—bits of a timer, some explosive, or even part of a car that the bomber used to transport the device. That sort of evidence is left inadvertently, usually because a bomber is convinced that the blast will obliterate any clues to his identity. In other cases, however, investigators occasionally find helpful information in communications that bombers purposely leave behind.

The Liberation Army

The 1993 World Trade Center bombing investigation provides a good example. Four days after the attack, the *New York Times* received a letter from a group calling itself "the fifth battalion in the Liberation Army." The group claimed responsibility for the bombing, and explained why they did it: "We, the fifth battalion in the LIBERATION ARMY, declare our responsibility for the explosion on the mentioned building. This action was in response to the American political, economical, and military support to Israel the state of terrorism and to the rest of the dictator countries in the region."[45] The letter went on to threaten more violence, claiming that there were 150 soldiers in the Liberation Army ready to continue their attacks unless the United States stopped its aid to Israel.

The letter, which was turned over to investigators by the *Times* staff, offered clear evidence that the attack was politically motivated. More importantly, however, although the letter was not signed by a specific individual, it ended up providing the identity of the writer.

Files from a computer used by Nidal Ayyad indicated his involvement in the 1993 bombing of the World Trade Center.

Retrieving Deleted Files

Mohammad Salameh was already a likely suspect in the World Trade Center bombing. Investigators had identified him as the renter of the vehicle that had transported the bomb to the underground garage. Detectives had been gathering information on Salameh's closest friends, thinking that they might have been coconspirators in the attack.

One of the men under surveillance was Nidal Ayyad, a research chemist at a company called Allied Signal. Ayyad was especially interesting to investigators, because as a chemist he had both the knowledge of how to build a bomb and access to the materials needed.

Mohammad Salameh was one of four men convicted of the 1993 bombing of the World Trade Center.

In their investigation of the Liberation Army letter, detectives seized Ayyad's computer at Allied Signal. Although Ayyad had tried to delete many of his files, technicians were able to take apart the computer's hard drive and recover them. As they scanned the deleted files, technicians found drafts of the Times letter, proving that it had been written on that computer.

By the Numbers

102

Number of mailbox bombings in the United States in 2004

Proof Positive

Additional evidence from the letter proved even more damning to Ayyad. In their examination of the original letter, technicians had done DNA swabs on both the stamp and the seal of the envelope. "Remember, DNA is present in saliva," says one forensic technician, "and that's one of the first things we test, whether it's present on a glass, the back of a stamp, even the mouthpiece of a telephone. If you are lucky enough to have a suspect to compare that DNA sample to, you could be in business."[46]

In this case, investigators took DNA samples from Ayyad as well as Salameh and two others believed to have been part of the conspiracy. Dave Williams, one of the lead investigators on the case, recalls how nervous Ayyad was when the technician was about to swab the inside of his cheek for a DNA sample.

"[C]ompared to the other suspects," he said, "when I touched Ayyad's mouth it was as dry as cotton, which is what happens when someone is extremely nervous. There was no question in my mind that the DNA test would confirm that Ayyad's saliva was on the envelope flap. That's what happened, proving he'd written and mailed the letter."[47]

Linguistic Analysis

Sometimes a bomber's communication provides clues that are not physical—like fingerprints or DNA—but rather are contained in the language of the message. Bombing investigators often submit any letters or other communications they receive to linguistic analysts who carefully examine the text. They pay special attention to the grammar, spelling, vocabulary, and style of the writing, for these things can sometimes offer hints about the bomber's background, level of education, and even whether English is his or her primary language. Even though bombers may attempt to mislead law enforcement agencies by "dumbing down" the language of a letter with incorrect grammar and spelling, there are often clues that are unmistakable.

Linguistic analysis was used in 2000 when a white church group was planning to help rebuild a black church that had been damaged by a fire in Virginia. The church group received letters threatening to firebomb the black church if they did so. The letters contained phrases referring to white supremacy, as well as racial epithets.

Investigators searched computer databases of phrases and vocabulary common to many hate groups throughout the United States. They found that wording in the letters matched literature distributed by two militant groups operating in Virginia and West Virginia. By narrowing down the suspects to members of these groups, investigators were able to locate the people who sent the letters before they could carry through on their threats.

Frustration over the Junkyard Bomber

The most famous case of a bomber being caught by his own words was that of Theodore Kaczynski, known as the Unabomber. He was responsible for killing 3 people and injuring 29 with 16 homemade bombs.

While investigators often recover clues from bomb fragments at the scene, this bomber confounded them. For one thing, there were almost no traceable elements in his bombs. In fact, they appeared to be totally homemade. Even fasteners and screws seemed as if he had fashioned them himself. He used wood and metal scraps, and he even was careful to remove labels from batteries, lest investigators try to trace them. Because most of the elements of his bombs were not store-bought, investigators privately referred to him as the Junkyard Bomber.

Investigators looking at the friends, associates, and coworkers of the victims were unable to find any name in common, either. "Most bombers are very open about their reason for their actions," says Jim Freedman, who headed the Unabomber Task Force. "They're mad at a particular corporation, or a particular person, . . . and from the investigative standpoint, you work that backwards as to who has a grudge against that company or that person."[48]

The Unabomber's Manifesto

Over eighteen years the Unabomber had targeted people at various universities and airlines with his bombs. Though the FBI and ATF were pouring money and manpower into the case, they had no leads until 1995. That was when the Unabomber went public, sending a thirty-five-thousand-word, sixty-five-page-long document to the *New York Times* and the *Washington Post*. Because he promised to kill more people unless it was printed, investigators allowed the newspapers to publish the document.

At first linguistic analysts learned little from the piece, which was known as the Unabomber Manifesto. In it the bomber argued that technology was ruining society and that people could never be productive or happy unless they returned to a simpler, computer-free existence. The grammar and vocabulary indicated that the writer was bright and well educated, but there were no clues to his identity. He was not part of a hate group, so the database found nothing familiar in his phrases and text.

For eighteen years, Theodore Kaczynski eluded capture in part because his bombs contained no traceable elements.

But a reader of the Unabomber Manifesto, Linda Patrik, saw something very familiar. She recognized some of the phrases in the document because she had often heard her brother-in-law, Theodore, use those same words. Patrik downloaded the manifesto and showed it to her husband, David Kaczynski.

Kaczynski agreed that the phrases were familiar and notified investigators. His brother was living a solitary existence in a cabin in the wilderness of Montana but was almost assuredly the author of the manifesto. Several of the phrases were familiar to David Kaczynski and his wife, but the one that stood out was "cool-headed logicians." Don Foster, a linguistic analyst who worked on the Unabomber case, recalls, "The entire [manifesto] was structured like a badly edited academic dissertation—or like one of Ted's angry letters from Montana. . . . David did not have to study the whole 35,000 word document

David Kaczynski contacted authorities when he recognized the words of his brother, Theodore, in the Unabomber Manifesto.

A Biological Bomb

Shrapnel is not the only "extra" that bomb makers could add to an explosive device. In fact, the threat of a bomb containing a payload of chemical or biological material that could kill or seriously injure thousands of people is a nightmare scenario for explosives experts. Since the mid-1990s, in fact, there have been more than a dozen close calls, where agents have been able to intercept the material before it was made into a bomb.

One of the most frightening occurred in November 1995, when a forty-three-year-old Nevada man named Larry Harris was arrested with a vial of an organism that causes the bubonic plague. Harris, a member of a white supremacist group called the Aryan Nation, had illegally filled out a state form permitting him to order the bacteria from a biomedical supply house. A mild explosive laced with the organism in a crowded city area could kill hundreds of thousands of people who would not realize the danger until they were infected.

from beginning to end. He had heard it all before, and he recognized the voice."[49]

Very soon after David Kaczynski alerted authorities, Theodore Kacynski was arrested. The case, say experts, might never have been solved if it had not been for the familiar phrases recognized by a family member.

"A Lot of People . . . Were Sure It Was Foreigners"

Sometimes a bomber's words are not necessary to identify him. However, they can be valuable for a number of other reasons. They may provide some explanation about the bomber's motive—something that may help investigators in future cases.

Timothy McVeigh, a decorated veteran, at first seemed an unlikely suspect in the Oklahoma City bombing.

Letters and other papers written by a bomber may also provide additional evidence that can strengthen the case against the suspect once it gets to trial.

In the case of the Oklahoma City bombing, many people were startled when they learned that the main suspect was McVeigh, a decorated veteran of the Persian Gulf war. "A lot of people around here were sure it was foreigners, most probably Middle East terrorists," says Steve, a pilot who lives in the Oklahoma City area. "It was definitely jumping to conclusions, I know, but it seemed a lot more believable than McVeigh, at least on the surface."[50]

When investigators began examining McVeigh's background, they found letters he had written that showed that he was furious with the actions of the federal government—especially the FBI and the ATF. He accused both of those agencies of sidestepping the Constitution in prosecuting American citizens.

McVeigh felt that citizens needed to fight back against a government that was taking their freedoms away. In one letter to his hometown newspaper in upstate New York, he wrote, "Do we have to shed blood to reform the current system? I hope it doesn't come to that! But it might."[51]

Part of the evidence against Timothy McVeigh came from letters in which he expressed his anger against the federal government.

Anger over Waco

Those who knew McVeigh confided that he was especially angry at the way the government handled the fifty-one-day siege at Waco, Texas, in 1993, after which government agents raided a compound occupied by a sect called Branch Davidians. Believing the sect was stockpiling automatic weapons, ATF agents tried to arrest the leader of the Davidians, David Koresh. Unwilling to surrender, Koresh and the Davidians stayed in their compound until the ATF finally shot tear gas inside and a fire broke out. Eighty-one Davidians, including seventeen children, were killed in the fire.

McVeigh wrote a letter to the ATF that was retrieved by investigators from his sister Jennifer's computer. In the letter he condemned the agency for its actions at Waco. "ATF," he warned, "all you tyrannical

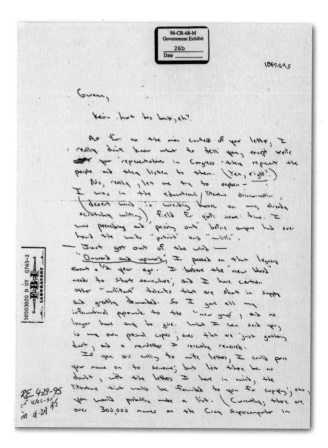

m——f——ers will swing in the wind one day for your trea-sonous actions against the Constitution and the United States."[52]

Most damning, however, was a letter McVeigh wrote to his sister a few months before the bombing, telling her that in April 1995, "something big is going to happen."[53] In light of his preoccupation with Waco, investigators realized, it was not surprising that McVeigh had chosen the date April 19 for the bombing at Oklahoma City—it was on April 19, 1993, that the Waco incident occurred.

Words from the Grave

Just as perplexing as McVeigh's involvement in the bomb-ing seemed at first were the motives of the four young sui-cide bombers in London. The four were what investigators call "clean skins," meaning that they had little in their back-grounds to raise suspicions. None had police or terrorist files, all came from middle-class backgrounds, and three of the four had grown up in Britain. Though they were all of Middle Eastern descent, they were all British citizens as well.

A video made by one of the bombers, however, provided investigators with an explanation for the attacks. The video was broadcast on the Arab network Al Jazeera on September 1, 2005, almost two months after the bombing. In it, Mohammed Sidique Khan, a thirty-year-old teacher of dis-abled elementary school students in London and father of two small children, explains why the attack was carried out. Westerners, he said, have failed to heed previous warnings, "therefore we will talk to you in a language you understand. Our words are dead until we give them life with our blood." He also threatened more catastrophes in retaliation for Britain's involvement with the United States in the war against Iraq—an invasion that he believed was unwarranted aggression against Muslim people. "I talk to you today about the blessed London battle," he said, "which came as a slap in the face of the tyran-nical, crusader British arrogance. It's a sip from the glass that the Muslims have been drinking from."[54]

Becoming a Document Examiner

Job Description:

A document examiner gathers, assesses, and maintains any paper evidence that is part of an investigation and performs any tests necessary to identify the way it was printed, written, or copied. The examiner also analyzes handwriting, grammar, vocabulary, and other clues that could help identify the person who wrote the document.

Document examiners play a key role in dealing with the paper evidence in bombings and other crimes.

Education:

The aspiring examiner must have a bachelor's degree from a college or university, with course work in forensic science, biology, chemistry, or criminalistics. After that, professional research and laboratory work alongside an experienced examiner is preferred by most agencies.

Qualifications:

A document examiner must be skilled in laboratory collection techniques as well as laws pertaining to the correct handling of criminal evidence. In addition, the examiner must be knowledgeable about analyzing inks, papers, business machines, and computers.

Salary:

Most entry-level document examiners earn between $50,000 and $58,000.

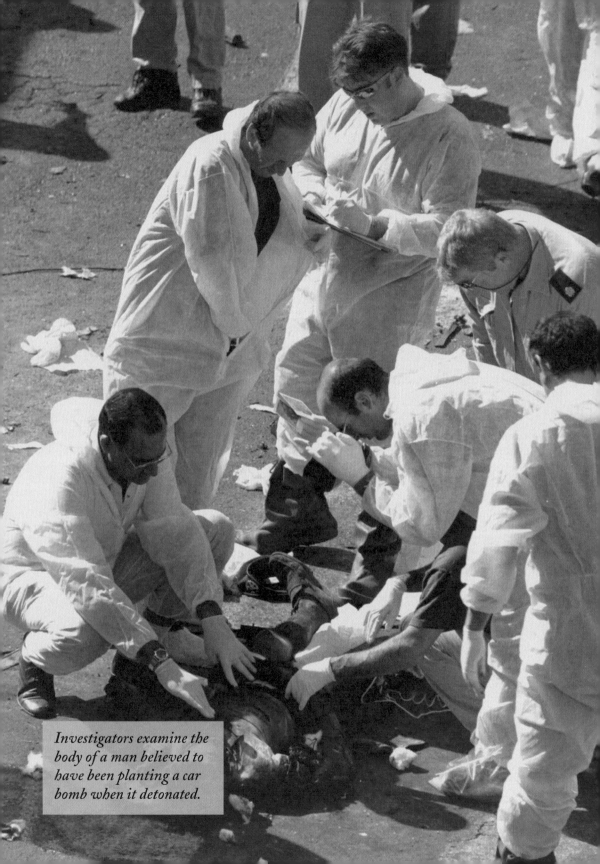

Investigators examine the body of a man believed to have been planting a car bomb when it detonated.

The Reality of Bombings

Experts concede that it is impossible to accurately predict bombings or to identify potential bombers. The differences among McVeigh, Moody, the London bombers, and Kaczysnski, for example, are far greater than any similarities among them. "It's meaningless to say that [bombers] are angry," says one psychologist. "Lots of people are angry about things, but fortunately, very few of them resort to building bombs."[55]

Some people, troubled by the increasing number of bombing incidents in the United States and around the world, suggest that stronger measures should be used to discourage bombings. They suggest that law enforcement conduct more searches of people in public places and that more sophisticated, high-tech scanners be developed that can detect the presence of explosives.

But even as these things are being considered, bomb experts say that the increasing number of bombings—particularly those of a terrorist nature—show that bombs are quite easily made and set off in cities around the world. It is a troubling fact of life in the twenty-first century that society will continue to need the skills of highly trained bombing investigators for some time to come.

Notes

Introduction: An Unspeakable Crime

1. Quoted in Clive Irving, ed., *In Their Name: Oklahoma City: The Official Commemorative Volume.* New York: Random House, 1995, pp. 34–35.

2. Nancy Gibbs, "The Blood of Innocents," *Time*, May 1, 1995, p. 56.

3. Ron Kelley, personal interview by author, Minneapolis, Minnesota, August 13, 2005.

4. Quoted on *CNN*, coverage of London bombing, July 7, 2005.

Chapter 1: Bombs from the Inside Out

5. Name withheld, personal interview by author, St. Paul, Minnesota, August 4, 2005.

6. Quoted in David Fisher, *Hard Evidence: How Detectives Inside the FBI's Sci-Crime Lab Have Helped Solve America's Toughest Cases.* New York: Simon & Schuster, 1995, p. 60.

7. Name withheld, August 4, 2005.

8. Quoted in Phillip Pina, "Pipe Bomb Suspect's Circuitous Route," *Seattle Times*, May 13, 2002, p. A4.

9. Name withheld, phone interview by author, August 3, 2005.

10. Kelley, interview.

Chapter 2: The Scene of the Bombing

11. Quoted in Fisher, *Hard Evidence*, p. 77.

12. Quoted in Irving, *In Their Name*, p. 89.

13. Quoted in S.F. Tomajczyk, *Bomb Squads.* Osceola, WI: MBI, 1999, p. 14.

14. Quoted in Fisher, *Hard Evidence*, p. 64.

15. Quoted in Tomajczyk, *Bomb Squads*, p. 15.

16. Quoted in Fisher, *Hard Evidence*, p. 68.

17. Name withheld, August 3, 2005.

18. Quoted in Jim Dwyer and David Kocieniewski, *Two Seconds Under the World.* New York: Crown, 1994, p. 84.

Chapter 3: Identifying the Dead

19. Dale, personal interview by author, Minneapolis, Minnesota, August 12, 2005.

20. Name withheld, August 3, 2005.

21. Danny Coulson, *No Heroes: Inside the*

FBI's Secret Counter-Terror Force. New York: Pocket Books, 1999, p. 488.

22. Quoted in Craig S. Smith, "Inches at a Time, Crews Search for Bodies in a London Tunnel," *New York Times*, July 11, 2005, p. 1.

23. Amy, personal interview by author, St. Paul, Minnesota, August 5, 2005.

24. Amy, interview.

25. Quoted on *CNN*, July 10, 2005.

Chapter 4: Working with the Evidence

26. Quoted in Philippe Naughton, "TATP Is Suicide Bombers' Weapon of Choice," *London Times online*, July 15, 2005. www.timesonline.co.uk/article/0>>22989-1695442,00.html.

27. Quoted in Fisher, *Hard Evidence*, p. 69.

28. Quoted in Steven Emerson and Brian Duffy, *The Fall of Pan Am 103: Inside the Lockerbie Investigation.* New York: G.P. Putnam's Sons, 1990, p. 152.

29. Quoted in Fisher, *Hard Evidence*, p. 69.

30. Quoted in Elizabeth Flynn, "Erin Bower Grows Up," *Indianapolis Woman Magazine*, April 2002. www.indianapoliswoman.com/covergallery/02/apr.htm.

31. Quoted in PBSonline, "Bombing of America," *Nova*, March 25, 1997. www.pbs.org/wgbh/nova/transcripts/2310tbomb.html.

32. Mick, personal interview by author, Minneapolis, Minnesota, August 1, 2005.

33. Fisher, *Hard Evidence*, p. 85.

34. Name withheld, August 3, 2005.

Chapter 5: Watchful Eyes

35. Quoted in Ian Cobain, "Attack on London: Suicide Bomb Theory After Anxious Passenger Report," *Manchester Guardian*, July 9, 2005, p. 5.

36. Quoted on *CNN*, July 15, 2005.

37. Coulson, *No Heroes*, p. 293.

38. Quoted in Coulson, *No Heroes*, p. 528.

39. Quoted in Fisher, *Hard Evidence*, p. 73.

40. Name withheld, telephone interview, August 4, 2005.

41. Quoted in "London Bombs: CCTV Can Find Guilty," *Birmingham Post*, July 12, 2005, p. 7.

42. Quoted in Jason Bennetto, "Hunt for the Bombers," *London Independent*, July 12, 2005, p. 9.

43. Quoted on *CNN*, July 9, 2005.

44. Quoted in David E. Kaplan and Thomas Grose, "On the Terrorists' Trail," *U.S. News & World Report*, July 25, 2005, p. 22.

Chapter 6: The Bomber's Own Words

45. Quoted in Dwyer and Kocieniewski, *Two Seconds Under the World*, p. 196.

46. Amy, interview.

47. Quoted in Fisher, *Hard Evidence*, p. 82.

48. Quoted in PBSonline, "Bombing of America."

49. Donald W. Foster, *Author Unknown: On the Trail of Anonymous*. New York: Henry Holt, 2000, p. 99.

50. Steve, phone interview by author, September 1, 2005.

51. Quoted in Coulson, *No Heroes*, p. 508.

52. Quoted in Coulson, *No Heroes*, p. 509.

53. Quoted in George Lane and Howard Pankratz, "Letters from McVeigh Hinted at 'Something Big,'" *Denver Post*, May 7, 1997, p. A1.

54. Quoted in Sally Buzbee, "Tape of London Bomber Surfaces," *Minneapolis Star Tribune*, September 2, 2005, p. A3.

55. Lynn, phone interview by author, September 1, 2005.

For Further Reading

Books

Allan Gerson and Jerry Alder, *The Price of Terror: Lessons of Lockerbie for a World on the Brink*. New York: HarperCollins, 2000. Excellent resource with very thorough index.

David Owen, *Hidden Evidence: Forty True Crimes and How Forensic Science Helped Solve Them*. Willowdale, ON: Firefly, 2000. Good photographs and very helpful accounts of the 1993 World Trade Center and 1995 Oklahoma City bombings.

Richard A. Serrano, *One of Ours: Timothy McVeigh and the Oklahoma City Bombing*. New York: Norton, 1998. Good information on McVeigh's background and motivation for the 1995 bombing.

Web Sites

ATF Online, "Arson and Explosives" (www.atf.treas.gov/explarson/index.htm). Recommended site, sponsored by the federal Bureau of Alcohol, Tobacco, Firearms, and Explosives with numerous links to discussion of types of explosives, antiterrorism teams, and a very interesting section on the Dipole Might program.

ATF Online, "Canines" (www.atf.treas.gov/kids/canines.htm). This site, designed as a special ATF Kids Page, is a colorful and interesting introduction to the role of dogs in bombing and arson investigation, in recovery of both victims and evidence.

CNN Interactive, "Oklahoma City Tragedy" (www.cnn.com/US/OKC). Excellent site with links covering the bombing, the rescue effort, the investigation, and the trial of the Oklahoma City bombers.

Works Consulted

Books

Danny Coulson, *No Heroes: Inside the FBI's Secret Counter-Terror Force*. New York: Pocket, 1999. Good inside information about the 1995 Oklahoma City bombing case.

Jim Dwyer and David Kocieniewski, *Two Seconds Under the World*. New York: Crown, 1994. Excellent section on the recovery of important evidence from the World Trade Center garage following the 1993 attack.

Steven Emerson and Brian Duffy, *The Fall of Pan Am 103: Inside the Lockerbie Investigation*. New York: G.P. Putnam's Sons, 1990. Very well written, readable account of the 1988 bombing and especially its effect on the citizens of Lockerbie, Scotland.

David Fisher, *Hard Evidence: How Detectives Inside the FBI's Sci-Crime Lab Have Helped Solve America's Toughest Cases*. New York: Simon & Schuster, 1995. Helpful section on explosives laboratory work.

Donald W. Foster, *Author Unknown: On the Trail of Anonymous*. New York: Henry Holt, 2000. Helpful informa-tion on the Unabomber case at an advanced reading level.

Clive Irving, ed., *In Their Name: Oklahoma City: The Official Commemorative Volume*. New York: Random House, 1995. Fine photographs and first-person accounts of the terrorist bombing that killed 168 people.

S.F. Tomajczyk, *Bomb Squads*. Osceola, WI: MBI, 1999. Very readable.

Periodicals

Jason Bennetto, "Hunt for the Bombers," *Independent* (London), July 12, 2005.

Sally Buzbee, "Tape of London Bomber Surfaces," *Minneapolis Star Tribune*, September 2, 2005.

Ian Cobain, "Attack on London: Suicide Bomb Theory After Anxious Passenger Report," *Guardian* (Manchester), July 9, 2005.

Nancy Gibbs, "The Blood of Innocents," *Time*, May 1, 1995.

David E. Kaplan and Thomas Grose, "On the Terrorists' Trail," *U.S. News & World*

Report, July 25, 2005.

George Lane and Howard Pankratz, "Letters from McVeigh Hinted at 'Something Big,'" *Denver Post*, May 7, 1997.

Phillip Pina, "Pipe Bomb Suspect's Circuitous Route," *Seattle Times*, May 13, 2002.

Post (Birmingham), "London Bombs: CCTV Can Find Guilty," July 12, 2005.

Craig S. Smith, "Inches at a Time, Crews Search for Bodies in a London Tunnel," *New York Times*, July 11, 2005.

Internet Sources

Elizabeth Flynn, "Erin Bower Grows Up," *Indianapolis Woman Magazine*, April 2002. www.indianapoliswoman.com/covergallery/02/apr.html.

Philippe Naughton, "TATP Is Suicide Bombers' Weapon of Choice," *Times* (London) *Online*, July 15, 2005. www.timesonline.co.uk/article/0,,22989-1695442,00.html.

PBS, "Bombing of America," *NOVA*. Originally aired March 25, 1997. www.pbs.org/wgbh/nova/transcripts/2310tbomb.html.

Index

Picture Credits

Cover: Getty Images

Maury Aaseng, 36, 63

© Gyori Antoine/CORBIS SYGMA, 90

© Associated Press/AP, 44, 70, 73, 79, 84

© Associated Press/FEDERAL EMER-GENCY MANAGEMENT AGE, 35

© Associated Press, Justice Department, 68, 69, 87

© Associated Press/PA, 18

© Associated Press, TIME/SABA, 7 (inset), 29

© Bettmann/CORBIS, 61

© Bloomberg/News/Landov, 66

© Custom Medical Stock Photo, 52

© Denver Post/Kent Meireis/CORBIS SYGMA, 83

© Dusko Despotovic/CORBIS, 62

© Dave Ellis/Pool/CORBIS, 59

© EPA/Landov, 67

© EPA/DYLAN MARTINEZ/POOL/Landov, 42

© Najlah Feanny/CORBIS SABA, 26

Getty Images, 38

© John Kuntz/Reuters/Landov, 23

Michael Maass, 89

© Jeff Moore/MAXPPP/Landov, 41

© Wally McNamee/CORBIS, 30

© Namil Mounzer/EPA/Landov, 32

Joseph Paris, 17

© Reuters/CORBIS, 19, 24, 51, 53, 55, 74, 80, 86

© Reuters/Alexander Demianchuk/Landov, 33

© MAIMAN RICK/CORBIS SYGMA, 12

© Damir Sagolj/Reuters/Landov, 49

© Science Source/Photo Researchers, 40

© Scotland Yard/Handout/Reuters/COR-BIS, 75, 77

© Greg Smith/CORBIS, 7

© Tek Image/Photo Researchers, 47

© Time Life Pictures/Getty Images, 56

© Sion Touhig/CORBIS, 9

Scott Weiss, 8

© Howard Yanes/Reuters/CORBIS, 14

About the Author

Gail B. Stewart received her undergraduate degree from Gustavus Adolphus College in St. Peter, Minnesota. She did her graduate work in English, linguistics, and curriculum study at the College of St. Thomas and the University of Minnesota. She taught English and reading for more than ten years.

She has written over ninety books for young people, including a series for Lucent Books called The Other America. She has written many books on historical topics such as World War I and the Warsaw ghetto.

Stewart and her husband live in Minneapolis with their three sons, Ted, Elliot, and Flynn; two dogs; and a cat. When Stewart is not writing, she enjoys reading, walking, and watching her sons play soccer.